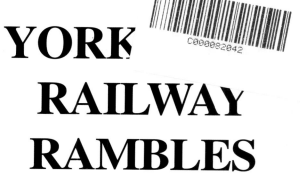

YORK RAILWAY RAMBLES

Volume 1: North and East

A guide to walking and cycling
through the railway history
of
North and East Yorkshire.
by
David F. Walford.

Illustrations
by
Peter White and Peter Steel.

Additional illustrations
and route maps
by
David F. Walford

SANTONA PUBLICATIONS
HULL
2000

Yorkshire Railway Rambles
Vol.1 North and East

First Published in 2000

Cover Illustrations by Steve Flint
Front. Stamford Bridge Viaduct
Back. Staintondale

British Library Cataloguing-in-Publication Data.
A catalogue record for this book is available from the British Library.
Copyright © 2000 by **David F. Walford.**

First Published in 2000 by,
Santona Publications.
Rydal Mount.
224 Marlborough Avenue.
Hull HU5 3LE.

Printed by The Amadeus Press, Bradford.

ISBN 0 9538448 0 3

Yorkshire Railway Rambles
Vol.1 North and East

In Memory of Mrs Olive Walford (1917-1997).
A remarkable woman, a wonderful mother.

Acknowledgements

With special thanks to my wife Sarah and
to Steve Flint, Peter White and Peter Steel
in the preparation of this book.

David F. Walford, July 2000.

The Spirit of Santona
Onward to the Horizon

SANTONA PUBLICATIONS
HULL

Frontispiece

Memories of Steam

Peter White

Foreword

This book is the latest work of knowledgeable and respected Yorkshire writer and railway historian, David F. Walford.

In his first book, Yorkshire Wolds Wanderings, he brought a fresh dimension to the exploration of the countryside. His unique approach was to combine the practicalities of country walking with a descriptive and definitive text which rekindled the rich historical heritage surrounding his chosen routes.

This first volume of Yorkshire Railway Rambles continues in the same style and genre.

David is an avid walker and keen cyclist in both his native county as well as further afield throughout the UK. Yet, despite his love of far off places in the Scottish Highlands, or amongst the Welsh hills, his passion and interest for his local area always enthuses from every word he writes.

Drawing inspiration from his engineering background and his strong family links with the railway companies that served the Yorkshire area, he has created this knowledgeable insight to help you to explore our once great railway heritage to the full.

Firstly he summarises the development of the Yorkshire railway system before going on to explain its steady decline in the twentieth century. He then moves on to explore, in much more detail, many of the dismantled lines that today you can enjoy on foot, by cycle and even on horseback.

The information is presented in a way to enable the choice of either short circular rambles - of as little as an hour's stroll - to full day treks walking or cycling over moorland or dale.

For illustrations, David has again drawn on the talents of Hull artist Peter Steel to provide sketches of track-side detail, whilst for recreating bygone scenes of trains steaming over Yorkshire lines he has commissioned the skilled and well known Howden based artist Peter White.

Together they have beautifully illustrated many of the areas covered by the book and their work complements David's own detailed route maps which give unrivalled guidance for treks into the countryside.

YORKSHIRE RAILWAY RAMBLES

Contents

Introduction

Following on from my last book, Yorkshire Wolds Wanderings, this second title has enabled me to combine my love of walking and cycling amidst the beautiful countryside of Yorkshire with my passion for railway history and heritage. Through these pages my aim is to guide you around parts of our once grand railway system in North and East Yorkshire and let you explore the many dales and rugged coastal areas that the old lines gave access to.

The routes I have chosen hold a special place in my affections. For most, I never had the pleasure of travelling along them by train and today, when I walk or cycle on them, my imagination is fired by visions of what it must have been like in those bygone days. Days when the local stopping train would amble by full of chattering schoolchildren or the daily goods would pause to shunt a wagon or two in the sidings. Perhaps my dreams are rose tinted, as surely life would have been harsh at times, but it is such reverie that draws me back time and again to these glorious places.

In describing the walks I have therefore included a lot of historical background information about the railways, all of which I hope will help to enhance your days out in this beautiful part of England.

You do not have to be an ardent rambler or fanatical outdoor enthusiast to follow these walks. Just a pleasant stroll along any of these old railway routes will provide relaxation, exercise and enjoyment and I am sure that you, like me, will become completely engaged by the history and atmosphere that surrounds them.

Today the magnificent earthworks of the old routes now blend so well into the landscape and open up access to many parts of this splendid county. In contrast though, the sight of railway dereliction often seems to reflect a great deal of wasted effort, such as the physical exertion and skill of building the track or the considerable sums of money that were poured into their construction. However, thanks to the endeavours of local organisations and authorities, these old lines now have a new lease of life as public rights of way. Though most are unlikely ever to see railway tracks again, the fact that the public can once more enjoy these routes must go some way to offset the seemingly huge waste of effort that was expended by our forefathers.

I hope that Yorkshire Railway Rambles will encourage readers to venture out into the countryside and discover these fine legacies from the great age of railways.

David F. Walford. June 2000.

LIST OF WALKS AND CYCLE ROUTES

LIST OF ILLUSTRATIONS

Chapter 1

A Legacy of Railway Tracks

For many thousands of years civilised man had known that the biggest resistance to moving a heavy load was the frictional force between the ground and the object to be moved. Overcome the friction and the object would glide along with only a fraction of the original effort needed. This principle had, of course, led to the fabled use of logs as rollers and then to the gradual development of the wheel.

By the time of the Industrial Revolution, this understanding of physical laws led to the development of inland waterways. Canals and water transport use the water itself to minimise the friction between the heavy load and the ground. Transport of bulky items and commodities by canal and waterway became fairly widespread in the late eighteenth and early nineteenth centuries. However, in many situations, canals were not always a versatile or cost effective option since they could take years to construct and were not very practical to build over difficult terrain. So the idea of using wheels to move objects over dry land came to the forefront of transport technology and the concept of a railway was born.

Whilst the true origins 'railways' are a matter of conjecture, it is generally accepted that in the latter part of the eighteenth century our forefathers began moving wagons loaded with heavy goods along pre-laid tracks. These early 'wagonways' used a crude form of track with

rails made of wood to guide the wooden wagon wheels along. Eventually it was found that an iron wheel on an iron rail was very free running and this combination eventually superseded all others.

Along with men, horses and ponies were used to pull the wagons over the rails and the logic of coupling two or three wagons together to form a train developed.

Concurrent with these early railways were inventions and developments in the field of mechanical power and the genius of several pioneering inventors saw the creation of the first crude steam engines. Firstly, these were stationary machines and were used to pump water (and thus drain shallow mine shafts), but could also be adapted to haul a few wagons along a railway by rope.

It was the next development that was to prove crucial. The steam engine was itself placed upon wheels and used as a locomotive to pull a rake of coupled wagons over an iron track. A few early steam locomotives were soon to be found operating within the confines of colliery railways. Puffing Billy, which ran at the Wylam Colliery in Newcastle is perhaps the most celebrated.

However, with the foresight of Britain's pioneering railway engineers, the enormous potential of the locomotive was grasped and further progress with designs occurred leading to their use on the first public railway between Stockton and Darlington in 1825.

The principle of railways was now firmly established and, just five years later, with the Rainhill locomotive trials and the opening of the Liverpool and Manchester Railway, the mobile steam engine was proclaimed as the motive power of the future.

The impact of railway development was remarkable and cannot be over-stressed. In just a few years this fundamental change in land transport had spread across the complete country and around the world. Railways became the most efficient means of overland travel known to mankind.

With the steady improvement of the steam locomotive and new processes in iron and steel manufacturing, the railway became king. People were no longer restricted to the speed and energy of a horse. In less than half a century over 100 tonnes could be moved at speeds up to 60 and 70mph (100km/h).

Railways spread rapidly in Britain in the first half of the nineteenth century and changed the shape of the landscape and the face of travel forever. From a horse and cart fumbling along a muddy track, taking several days to travel between Leeds and Hull, to the speed and bulk of a train gliding along the iron rails and speeding through tunnels, cuttings and over amazing bridges and viaducts!

It is perhaps no coincidence that Yorkshire and the North East of England found itself at the heart of early railway development. Under this often rugged countryside were large deposits of coal, iron ore, limestone and chalk; all vital ingredients for the up and coming new age of industrialisation.

Ports, both inland and coastal, were developing too. The requirement to move heavy goods and minerals around the county was considerable and it is perhaps the coming of the railways which provided the ignition for the Industrial Revolution. Without the railways the Industrial Revolution may never have happened.

Although the first railways tended to link mining areas with foundries or inland ports, the expanding towns and cities were soon to realise the enormous potential that a railway link could offer. The sea-going ports, such as Hull and Whitby, were early candidates for connection to the inland manufacturing centres. By the mid nineteenth century, the more far-sighted Victorian entrepreneurs saw the need to link many of these independent lines together and form a national network of railways connecting almost every population centre.

So began a dramatic period of railway history. Many routes were planned and though many were fanciful and came to nothing, others that often meandered over sparsely populated areas of countryside actually got built. Other railway projects of this era saw the duplication of routes, very often for political reasons, as one independent railway company would not wish to share its business with a rival. As such, when the twentieth century dawned, Britain had around 20,000 miles (32,000km) of railways crammed into this small island.

Yet with virtually no competition, other than a horse and cart, even the country branch line station was seen as the most important part of any town or village. If the railway was not there, little wealth could be created. No new mills could be built or mine shafts sunk if the powerful railway companies would not agree to construct a new line linking them to the rest of the massive network.

The accompanying map shows the many railways which criss-crossed Yorkshire just before the First World War. This Edwardian period is generally accepted as the heyday of the British Railway age, but sadly, from then on, a steady and unremitting decline took hold.

Yorkshire Railway Rambles 1. North and East

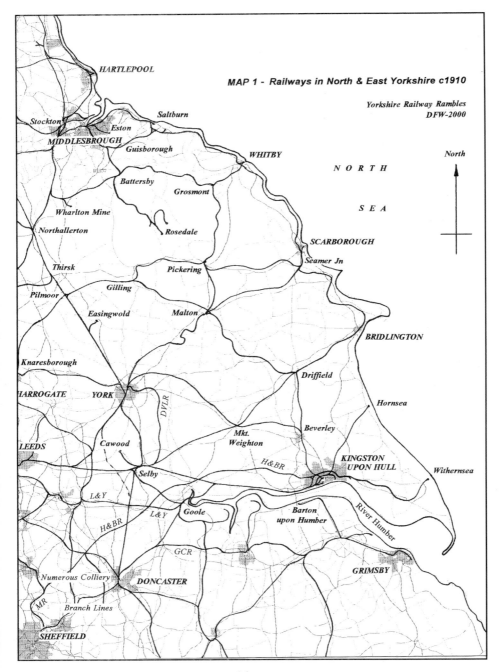

MAP 1 - Railways in North & East Yorkshire c1910

Yorkshire Railway Rambles
DFW-2000

North

HARTLEPOOL

Stockton
Eston
Saltburn
MIDDLESBROUGH
Guisborough
WHITBY

N O R T H

Battersby
Grosmont

S E A

Wharlton Mine
Northallerton
Rosedale
SCARBOROUGH

Thirsk
Pickering
Seamer Jn

Pilmoor
Gilling
Easingwold
Malton

BRIDLINGTON

Knaresborough
Driffield

HARROGATE
YORK
DVLR
Hornsea

LEEDS
Cawood
Mkt. Weighton
Beverley

KINGSTON UPON HULL
Withernsea

Selby
H&BR

L&Y
L&Y
Goole
Barton upon Humber
River Humber

H&BR
GCR

Numerous Colliery
DONCASTER
GRIMSBY

MR
Branch Lines
SHEFFIELD

A Legacy of Railway Tracks

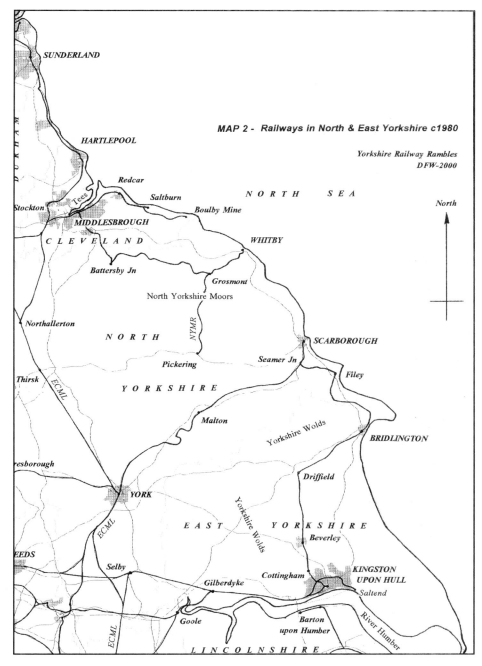

MAP 2 - Railways in North & East Yorkshire c1980

Yorkshire Railway Rambles
DFW-2000

SUNDERLAND

DURHAM

HARTLEPOOL

Redcar

Saltburn

NORTH SEA

Stockton

Tees

Boulby Mine

North

MIDDLESBROUGH

CLEVELAND

WHITBY

Battersby Jn

Grosmont

North Yorkshire Moors

NYMR

Northallerton

NORTH

SCARBOROUGH

Thirsk

ECML

Pickering

Seamer Jn

Filey

YORKSHIRE

Malton

Yorkshire Wolds

BRIDLINGTON

resborough

Driffield

YORK

ECML

Yorkshire Wolds

EAST YORKSHIRE

Beverley

LEEDS

Selby

Cottingham

KINGSTON
UPON HULL

Gilberdyke

Saltend

ECML

Goole

Barton
upon Humber

River Humber

LINCOLNSHIRE

So what happened? The arrival of the internal combustion engine is widely regarded as the key factor, it changed the face of twentieth century as dramatically as the railways had changed the face of the century before. The motor car and lorry proved to be a far more versatile form of land transport and soon reached out into all areas. With the steady encroachment of roads, the rural railways became less and less economical and, starting as long ago as the 1920s, services ceased and lines began to close.

Soon the closure of an uneconomical railway line became the norm, although the reduction in the railway system had different effects throughout the country. Most large cities had several duplicating routes from the nearest population centres and the loss of some of these railway lines was not necessarily felt so harshly. However, in rural areas, as at small coastal towns, the removal of the trains was much like a bereavement.

Following the Beeching Report of 1963 the process of railway closures swept the country at a speed few would have thought possible. In particular the closures cut a swathe through the rural branch and secondary lines, many of which ran through some of the most idyllic and picturesque parts of the countryside. The rural lines of Yorkshire being no exception.

After just a few short years thousands of miles of nineteenth century engineering was left to rot. The sight of derelict railway lines became almost more prolific than those still in use. Yet whilst many of these old lines were to be lost forever; under new roads schemes, housing and industrial estates, or even back to agriculture use, some were to be saved to become havens for walkers, cyclists and lovers of nature.

Generally the railways that closed prior to the Beeching era of the 1960s were the most uneconomical rural lines. The land was quickly sold back to large country estates or local farmers and one side of the railway boundary would rapidly disappear allowing the railway strip to become part of the adjoining field.

Where a railway had run through a cutting, in some cases, it was turned over to landfill, with refuse and rubbish being dumped to gradually back fill the area. Old embankments would erode, or be sold off as hard core, often for use on new road schemes in the area.

The closure of lines in the 1960s included some principle routes serving urban areas. Here the land would have a high value and was sold off for development before nature had a chance to reclaim it.

Many ring roads follow the course of dismantled railway lines today and shopping centres and trading estates have devoured old station sites and marshalling yards. Fortunately however, a few far sited councils successfully purchased complete railway routes from this round of closures and since then they have been steadily developed into public bridleways. Today these are rural sanctuaries where nature can flourish and the public can walk or cycle over the generally level ground that was once pounded by mighty steam trains.

In some instances overgrown public paths running alongside a railway boundary were transferred onto the course of the old trackbed. In other areas, short diversions were created to allow the removal of bridges and other structures that required expensive maintenance.

As I describe the routes of a selection of these new rights of way, so I will catalogue the key elements of the history of each railway line through the pages of this book. We will discover when and why the railway was built, how it developed prior to the reduction in traffic, followed by closure then rebirth as a new bridleway or footpath.

Climbing Enthorpe Bank c.1950s

Chapter 2

The Unfolding of Yorkshire's Railway Trails

The story of the development of Yorkshire's railway network is a reflection of the development of the County's mineral resources and navigable rivers. As covered in the previous chapter, the earliest requirement for a new transport system was to move coal and ore from the mines to the new industrial centres and iron foundries. As the Industrial Revolution took hold the effect became cyclical; more industry required more coal, more iron, more goods, and so on, all driving the need for more efficient transport. Likewise greater port and harbour capacity was needed to export finished products and import further raw materials.

By the middle of the nineteenth century all the towns in the West Riding were linked by railway to the ports on the east coast and to the expanding coal fields in South Yorkshire. Sheffield and Middlesbrough emerged as leading centres in the iron and steel industry, being followed later by Scunthorpe in the twentieth century. The major railway routes between these localities were thus established early on and most are still in use to this day.

Linking Yorkshire with Lancashire mill towns and the west coast meant a difficult battle to construct lines over and through the Pennines and six different routes eventually emerged. Many of those routes have now closed, being left for use by the rambler, as the next volume in this series will uncover.

Meanwhile within Yorkshire itself, many of the routes to the North, South and East came under the control of George Hudson, the infamous "Railway King", who jealousy guarded his territory which was centred on York.

By the mid nineteenth century many small railway companies had amalgamated with larger rivals and the map of Britain became carved up into territories often dominated by just one large company. Yorkshire, was indeed a case in point, with all rail travel through the North East of England being monopolised by the North Eastern Railway Company. The NER, formed by the merging of three companies on 31st July 1854, had its headquarters in York and took control of all the major routes to the east of the Pennines along with many of the smaller railways and dock companies. Only in the south and west of the county did competition exist with companies like the

Lancashire and Yorkshire Railway, the Midland Railway, the Great Central Railway and the London and North Western Railway having direct access.

During the latter part of the nineteenth century some small independent companies were formed to build secondary lines within NER territory, but most usually ended up selling their newly completed railway, at great financial loss to the promoters, to the all powerful North Eastern. Privately owned collieries often promoted new lines, but again, it was to the North Eastern they had to look for access to the main line railways.

As the massive industrialisation of South and West Yorkshire continued apace, more railway routes were opened and large scale docks were developed around the Humber and Tees. At Hull and Grimsby, the existing docks were greatly extended (The dock frontage onto the River Humber at Hull eventually covering over 7 miles (10km) by 1914.), whilst new ports, such as at Immingham and Goole, were built by the railway companies on completely new sites.

Although activities associated with industry and commerce were the key factors in the development of the railways, the carriage of passengers also played a significant, if perhaps secondary, role. The spa towns and east coast holiday resorts were to flourish as the railways delivered their visitors in droves during the summer season. Indeed, the resorts of Saltburn, Whitby, Scarborough, Bridlington, Hornsea and Withernsea all owe their rapid growth to the coming of the railways.

However, it should be remembered that it was the all-year-round goods traffic which provided the majority of revenue for the railways. Outside the growing London commuter belt, most people lived very close to their place of work, so a long train journey was often only a once-a-year summer holiday thrill for many of the working classes. The consequence of this was that so many seemingly 'well used' passenger railway routes became unprofitable after road haulage had robbed them of regular revenue and closure, even before the years of mass car ownership, was inevitable.

Ironically today, the opposite is true, as many surviving lines are virtually passenger routes in their entirety, with little or no goods traffic to speak of.

In the rural areas of Yorkshire, agriculture benefited from the arrival of railways in that produce and livestock could be moved more quickly to market. Exclusive to rural areas were a number of private 'light' railways that were constructed, mainly at the turn of the twentieth century. One example was the Derwent Valley Railway and such lines often took a meandering route between two larger market towns already served by the North Eastern Railway.

So it was that by Edwardian times the railway map of Yorkshire was, more or less, as complete as it would ever be. From then on, the slow but steady decline in railway activity would take place and leave operational railway routes as mere shadows of their former selves. It is perhaps a sad irony that the railways had to disappear so that we can now explore and enjoy their trackbeds and trails at leisure.

The unfolding of Yorkshire's railway trails, rising phoenix like from the ashes, was to take many years and, apart from some obvious exceptions, such as the Rosedale Ironstone lines, it was amongst the lightly used rural routes that the first closures occurred.

This became particularly acute after the Second World War as the motor coach and lorry started to take over a large slice of the rural transport work load.

In addition, with the nationalisation of the railways by the Labour Government in 1948, close attention was paid to duplicated routes and main lines between large centres of population. The need for economies ruled the closure of such lines, the largest of these being the former Great Central Railway main line from London to South Yorkshire and Lincolnshire.

In the area covered by this book, perhaps the most celebrated duplicated route was that of the Hull and Barnsley Railway. East Yorkshire had been dominated been the NER for many years and its main route into Hull followed a level course without any significant earthworks along the north bank of the River Humber. By contrast the almost parallel route of the old H&BR had to contend with mile after mile of steep gradients, deep chalk cuttings and three long tunnels through the chalk hills of the Wolds.

Such lines as these required hefty maintenance bills to keep the bridges, tunnels, cuttings and embankments in good order. Under the common ownership of British Railways, it was a straightforward task to install a few connecting spurs and then easily divert traffic onto other lines. Indeed, traffic could be deliberately re-routed to show that the route was operating at a substantial loss. Inevitable closure would, no doubt, soon follow.

Goods Train at Drewton Tunnel

Many rural and duplicate railway routes steadily closed throughout the 1950s, but it was following the 1963 Beeching Report that the most controversial closures occurred. In just a few short years the branch line and secondary routes in our chosen area had been decimated. Ironically the foundation for Yorkshire's railway trails had been laid.

The period of continuous closures faded at the end of the 1960s. Although several railway lines were still to go, and others remained under the threat of closure, wholesale closure had been slowed. Campaigning transport groups were formed and got their act together to create a formidable rearguard action against further closures.

By the 1980s there were moves to reopen stations for commuters in some heavily congested urban areas. Indeed, this initiative was accorded some success and even some brand new stations were built on new sites. In 1994 the British railway network was privatised, and despite much political opposition to the principle, new opportunities and railway facilities are being actively considered in many areas.

The rush to close further railway lines seems to have been halted and even reversed for the time being. Whether we will see a return of trains to the dismantled railway lines, no one can predict. Realistically, it is rather unlikely since the routes they follow are not important lines of communication today. Perhaps then, the route miles of Yorkshire's railway trails have now reached their apogee.

Let us now explore them.

Chapter 3

Planning Your Treks

Although it may seem unlikely that you would ever become lost whilst wandering along the trackbed of a derelict railway line, it is still very advisable to have a fundamental understanding of map reading and to be aware of all the possible problems that you could encounter in the countryside. Such knowledge will ensure your safety and welfare and greatly enhance your days out in the countryside.

Also, it is important that you should be fully familiar with all the different categories of rights of way and have a basic understanding of the country code.

Please spend a little time looking at the tips on the next few pages and then be fully equipped for your days out in the country.

Throughout this book I have included a series of detailed route maps of the old railway trails together with further guidance on making your rambles into circular walks wherever possible. The maps are meant as a guide only and it is strongly advised that you take with you the appropriate Ordnance Survey sheet for the area.

All the information on the maps in this book are drawn from my own records and whilst every effort is made to ensure that the information is correct at the time of going to press, the marking of a path or track is no guarantee of a right of way. In addition, some private lanes and paths, where there is no right of access, are marked only to help you to establish your exact location.

Generally all public rights of way are quite well indicated with signposts being provided by the local council. If a route is indicated as a 'Footpath', you can only walk along it, it is not for cycling or horse riding, and styles are provided for getting over fences.

On a route marked as a 'Bridleway', in addition to walking, you can take your bike or go on horseback and gates will be provided at fences rather than styles.

On a Green Lane (a road that has not been surfaced) you can technically take any vehicle. A good user of such a route will have the greatest respect for the fragile nature of the countryside and be aware that the passage of four wheel drive vehicles, if driven without care, can erode the surface and leave marks for many months.

With railway walks you will often come across the term 'Permissive Bridleway' or 'Permitted Path'. This is significant in that the route does not necessarily form part of a definitive right of way. It is private land (possibly in the ownership of the local authority) that can have restrictions placed on the access at any time. Keep a lookout for any notices posted, as parts of the trail may be closed for safety work or nature conservation. Such work is usually undertaken with the long term interests of the trail in mind.

Even if you are going out for just a couple hours, I always recommend that a few essential 'supplies' are taken with you in a rucksack (not a hand held bag). A few spare clothes, your trusty waterproofs, a little food, some chocolate bars and drinks. Also, along with my OS maps, I always carry a whistle, a compass and a few simple items of first aid.

Quite simply, the further you are going to wander from a centre of population, the more you need to plan and prepare for your day in the countryside. It is nothing more than common sense really, but good preparations will give you peace of mind should the weather change for the worse or difficulties arise. A mobile phone can also be invaluable in summoning assistance, but there are still many pockets within the countryside where reception is poor. Even today, with the wonders of GPS technology it is still well worth getting into a good preparatory routine!

Now to the Ordnance Survey maps. You do not have to be a fanatic like myself, with over two thousand bulging from my bookshelves, but the investment in a few good quality OS maps of the areas you regularly walk or ride over will be invaluable. For the maps that cover this part of Yorkshire, the illustration opposite indicates the OS sheet reference number

For hiking and rambling, the most popular OS map series is the Landranger Series. They are to a scale of 1:50 000 (1.25 inches to the mile) and are a good all purpose maps and each cover a large areas of the county.

For greater detail, the Pathfinder Series or the Outdoor Leisure and Explorer Series can be purchased. These maps are to a scale of 1:25 000 (2.5 inches to the mile) and rather more information and detail can be seen.

Reading these types of map is not especially difficult and certainly is only a little more complicated than following the average road atlas. Get accustomed to the various features on the map by spending some time looking at a view with the map open in your hand. Recognise

Planning Your Treks

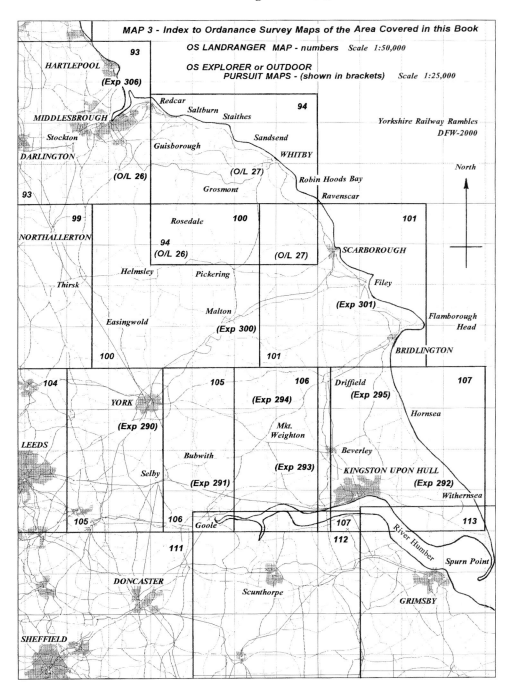

MAP 3 - Index to Ordanance Survey Maps of the Area Covered in this Book

OS LANDRANGER MAP - numbers *Scale 1:50,000*

OS EXPLORER or OUTDOOR
PURSUIT MAPS - (shown in brackets) *Scale 1:25,000*

Yorkshire Railway Rambles
DFW-2000

HARTLEPOOL

93

(Exp 306)

Redcar
Saltburn
Staithes

94

MIDDLESBROUGH

Sandsend

Stockton

Guisborough

WHITBY

DARLINGTON

North

(O/L 26)

(O/L 27)

Robin Hoods Bay

93

Grosmont

Ravenscar

99

Rosedale

100

101

NORTHALLERTON

94
(O/L 26)

(O/L 27)

SCARBOROUGH

Helmsley

Pickering

Thirsk

Filey

Malton

(Exp 301)

Easingwold

(Exp 300)

*Flamborough
Head*

100

101

BRIDLINGTON

104

105

106

Driffield

107

York

(Exp 294)

(Exp 295)

Hornsea

(Exp 290)

Mkt.
Weighton

LEEDS

Bubwith

Beverley

(Exp 293)

KINGSTON UPON HULL

Selby

(Exp 291)

(Exp 292)

Withernsea

105

106

Goole

107

113

111

112

River Humber

DONCASTER

Spurn Point

Scunthorpe

GRIMSBY

SHEFFIELD

how the various land marks are shown on the map and see how the contours (lines which indicate land of equal height) of the map describe type of terrain. As with virtually all mapping, the convention is to have North at the top, so with the aid of a compass to indicate which way North is, the correct orientation of a map can easily be established.

In the 'Fact File' panels which accompany each recommended walk I have quoted Grid References. These are simply a series of letters and numbers which define a specific point on a map. A simple example of how to use the grid reference is shown on all OS maps in the lower right corner. Remember to read the 'Easting' first, (along the bottom of the map), followed by the 'Northing' second (along the side of the map).

Although such map reading skills will not be required on many of these walks, it is always invaluable knowledge that may one day get you out of a difficult situation. Such map reading skills will also enable you to seek out other circular routes of your own, perhaps away from the busier areas, and search for that peace and tranquillity that most people yearn on their days spent in the countryside.

All distances given in this book are quoted in metric. OS maps have been in metric for many years now and the international system

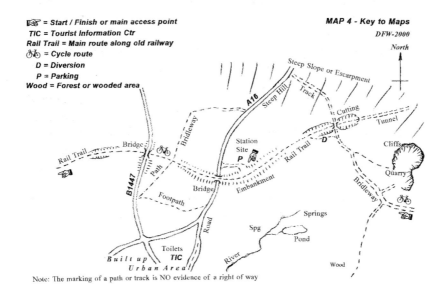

Note: The marking of a path or track is NO evidence of a right of way

is taught exclusively in schools. If you are more at home with imperial measurements then remember a couple of simple conversions; 1 metre (1m) is just over three feet (39 inches). 8 kilometres (8km) is equal to 5 miles. An OS map is divided into 1km squares, so a quick guide to the length of your route is to count the number of grid lines crossed (i.e. at least 1km will be travelled for every grid line crossed). At the end of each route described in this book, the 'Fact File' gives a brief account of the main points such as start and finish location, length of walk, typical time, map numbers, etc.

Most walkers and cyclists will be fully familiar with the country code. This prompts everyone to show a healthy respect for the countryside and for the people that live along the routes of public rights of way, or look to the land for their livelihood. Of particular significance with the walks in this book is that many old railway buildings, particularly country stations, have been sold and are now private residences. Such owners will naturally appreciate a respect for their privacy.

A number of the railway routes I have described cross over National Park land or National Trust property. Here it is especially important to be fully aware of the fragile nature of the area and avoid any accidental damage to flora and fauna.

If you take a dog, be aware that some of these areas have strict restrictions about the control and access of domestic animals, such as on the moors at lambing times.

If you are on a cycle, be aware that others on foot may not hear you approaching. Also your cycle may need checking carefully both before and after use. The vibration caused by riding over an old railway route may result in damage to your machine. When the trek described is designated as a footpath only I have highlighted, where possible, an alternative route for bikes. Naturally you can cover a far greater distance on a cycle than by foot, so with good use of the OS maps you can link up quiet country lanes with different bridleways to form longer circular routes.

The map overleaf shows the complete area covered by this book and can be used as an index to find the walk you want.

Yorkshire Railway Rambles 1. North and East

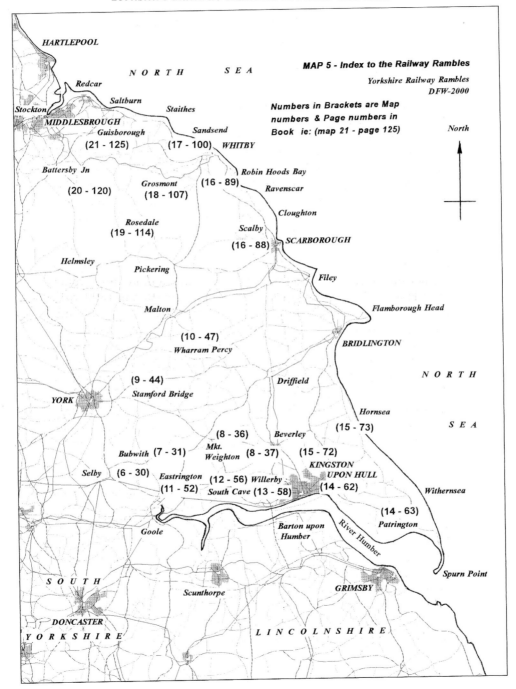

HARTLEPOOL

N O R T H   *S E A*

MAP 5 - Index to the Railway Rambles

Yorkshire Railway Rambles
DFW-2000

Redcar

Saltburn

Stockton

Staithes

Numbers in Brackets are Map
numbers & Page numbers in
Book ie: (map 21 - page 125)

North

MIDDLESBROUGH

Guisborough

Sandsend

(21 - 125)

(17 - 100) *WHITBY*

Battersby Jn

Robin Hoods Bay

Grosmont **(16 - 89)** Ravenscar

(20 - 120) **(18 - 107)**

Cloughton

Rosedale
(19 - 114)

Scalby

SCARBOROUGH

(16 - 88)

Helmsley

Pickering

Filey

Malton

Flamborough Head

(10 - 47)

Wharram Percy

BRIDLINGTON

(9 - 44)

Stamford Bridge

Driffield

N O R T H

YORK

Hornsea

(15 - 73)

S E A

(8 - 36) Beverley

Bubwith **(7 - 31)** Mkt.
Weighton **(8 - 37)** **(15 - 72)**

Selby **(6 - 30)** Eastrington **(12 - 56)** Willerby **KINGSTON UPON HULL**

(11 - 52) South Cave **(13 - 58)** **(14 - 62)**

Withernsea

(14 - 63)

Goole

Barton upon Humber

River Humber Patrington

Spurn Point

S O U T H

Scunthorpe

GRIMSBY

DONCASTER

Y O R K S H I R E

L I N C O L N S H I R E

Chapter 4

Around the Heart of The Wolds

Walk 1: THE BUBWITH TRAIL.

When it was first opened as a public railway, way back in 1847-48, the single track line between Selby and Market Weighton was very much a rural back water. Although Selby had been connected to Leeds in 1836, and to Hull in 1840, Market Weighton had only just been linked to the growing railway network by a line to York in 1846.

In the early years of operation there were approximately four trains per day each way which stopped at all stations along the route.

As yet no railway lines were open over the chalk hills of the Yorkshire Wolds that stood to the east of Market Weighton. Indeed it was to be many years before the status of the town grew to be an important railway junction. This finally began with the opening of a further line to Beverley in 1860, thus providing a more direct route from Hull to York, and was followed thirty years later, in 1890, by a link to Driffield, thereby giving a direct connection between South and West Yorkshire and the growing East Coast holiday resorts.

Although this line was built many years after the 'railway mania' period, it was opened by an independent company, the Market Weighton and Driffield Railway, with the grand intention of constructing a railway that would link the east coast at Bridlington with the recently opened Hull and Barnsley Railway (1885) via a junction in the Howden area. However, like so many grand schemes of that era, only a short section was ever built and it was soon absorbed by its big brother, the North Eastern Railway Company.

The effect of the Driffield link did however promote a significant increase in through traffic on the Selby to Market Weighton line. This was especially so during the summer holiday months in later years and in anticipation of this, the single track was doubled throughout. Had this not happened, then perhaps the railway may have closed well before the Beeching era of the early sixties. As part of that infamous plan, the line did eventually close in 1965, along with the other routes into Market Weighton, thereby taking the town off the railway map for good.

The origins of the bridleway from Bubwith to the south west of Market Weighton lie in a further grand transport plan that also never came to fruition. The main trunk road that duplicated the work of the railway, the A163, (now re-numbered A614), has long been accepted as totally inadequate to take the necessary volume of heavy lorries and holiday traffic. As such a significant length of the railway track bed was purchased by the then County Council, with the idea being to re-route the trunk road along this direct level line.

Without doubt, had this proposal not been on the drawing board, the railway land would have been quickly sold off piecemeal fashion to the local land owners. Most of it would then have reverted back to farming in this mainly agricultural area.

After may years of gathering dust, the plans for building a completely new trunk road slipped quietly away, rather like the plan for linking Bridlington with the Hull and Barnsley Railway had done one hundred years earlier. By the late 1970s the value of such stretches of derelict railway lines was being viewed in a different light. A far less expensive proposal to convert the trackbed into a walking and cycle route, and also provide a haven for nature, was put forward. This won the day and the route we now know was gradually opened on a peice-meal basis. The map on the next page guides you along the complete route and highlights adjoining rights of way and country lanes that link to it.

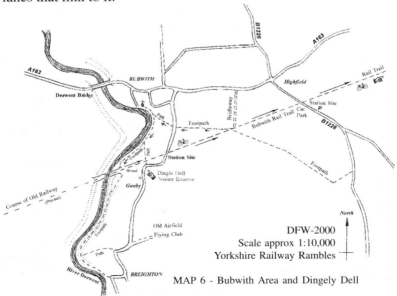

MAP 6 - Bubwith Area and Dingely Dell

Around the Heart of The Wolds

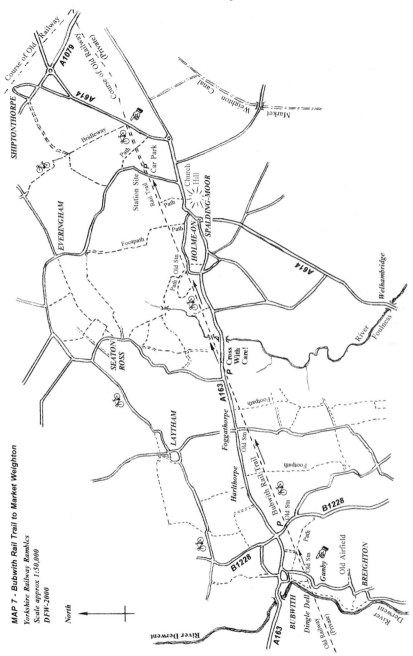

MAP 7 - Bubwith Rail Trail to Market Weighton
Yorkshire Railway Rambles
Scale approx 1:50,000
DFW-2000

North

As a result of the areas topography, the old railway is remarkably straight and has few notable engineering features along the part of the route covered here. To the west, several key navigable rivers had to be crossed whilst to the east, the rising hills of the chalk Wolds present a few difficulties to the railway engineers. You can start the walk or cycle ride at any of the many points marked on the map, but the following description of the route starts from Bubwith, in the west and leads to a point 4km SW from Market Weighton in the east.

The village of Bubwith lies 10km north, north east of Selby on the A163, with Howden around 9km to the south along the B1228. The thirteen century All Saints Church stands in a beautiful setting to the west of the village and close to the River Derwent.

The original settlement at Bubwith developed because of a river crossing built here many centuries ago although no historical remnants exist today.

The River Derwent was an important navigable waterway during the last century, giving access for boats up to the Pocklington canal. It also drains a vast area of North and East Yorkshire with its origins just a few kilometres away from the North Sea near to Scarborough. However, it actually flows west then south on its long journey to join the River Ouse and then the Humber, before eventually reaching the sea after many kilometres. Despite modern methods of control, the river is still notorious for flooding and after prolonged heavy rain on the North Yorkshire Moors much of the land surrounding the river ends up under water. Particularly damaging floods occurred in March 1999 when Malton and Stamford Bridge suffered disastrously.

Our walk starts 500 metres down stream at the point where the railway originally crossed the river. The point is accessed by a footpath along the river bank. The original railway bridge was a rather crude wooden and cast-iron structure. It had to be extensively rebuilt following a fire in August 1858 when the western approach viaduct was completely destroyed. This was not an uncommon occurrence on early railways, with hot cinders and ash falling from locomotives onto wooden structures, fires often took hold along the lines. With the new structure, brick arches replaced the original timber and these can still be seen today.

The main cast-iron span however has been demolished. An easily spotted change in the brickwork indicates where the line was widened at the south side to accommodate the second track in 1890.

The name of Dingle Dell is given to the nature reserve that forms the first part of the walk along the former trackbed from the river and the old station site. This green area is home to many flowers and wildlife and dogs should be kept on a lead in this area. It is a very overgrown area and is not suitable for cycles until Breighton Road is crossed by the old station buildings.

The route now follows a straight line to the east, north east. At several locations access may be gained to minor roads along the route. The next old station site to be passed is Highfield at the crossing with the B1228, and only 1.5km from Bubwith station. A small car park is available here and a public house for refreshment. It is 3km over the flat agricultural plain to the next station at Foggathorpe and the nearby old Black Swan village inn. Another 2km further east is the crossing point on the A163 where additional car parking is available. This road can be particularly busy in the summer months so be alert and take care.

With the crossing of the River Foulness 1km beyond the A163, Holme-on-Spalding-Moor appears on your left along with the station site and some nearby refreshments. This large village extends over 2km to the south east of the trek and has the distinctive Church Hill rising 40 metres above the flat plain. Although not high at 40 metres, because of the flatness of the surrounding area the effect is most striking with the tower of All Saints Church dominant on the summit. As you will see from the map, several footpaths give you options to make your own circular route in this area. Continuing along our track, the last station site to be passed is at Harswell, just beyond the minor road where another small car park has also been provided.

Harswell is only a small hamlet to the north of the line and in later years this station took the name of Everingham, a larger estate village 3km north west of Harswell. Like many of the stations on the Selby to Market Weighton line, the platforms were staggered, with one at each side of the road crossing. The reason for this configuration may be due to the doubling of the tracks which happened over forty years after the line was first opened. By that time, goods sidings may have occupied the required area opposite the main station buildings and platform, so it was thus logical and cheaper to provide the new platform further along the line.

It is now just 1km further along the trail to the old crossing with the A614 trunk road. At this point our route must unfortunately terminate. We are still 3km from Market Weighton and without a public path to take you directly into the town. As the original county council plan was to build a new road, no requirement was seen to purchase the last few kilometres of the trackbed beyond the trunk road. the remnants of the old line here have been turned back to agriculture. A bridleway does head north to give you a possible circular route back to the village of Harswell.

Fact File - The Bubwith Trail

Start/Finish: Dingle Dell (Bubwith) to Harswell.
Grid Refs: SE 711356 & SE 840405.
A flat straight railway without engineering features.
Location: 1km south of Bubwith on road to Breighton & Wressle to A614 3km south of Shiptonthorpe Roundabout, (car park at old station site 1km to the west near the hamlet of Harswell).
Max. length of walk: 14km (9 miles),
typical walking time 4 hours, one way.
Length of shorter walk: Dingle Dell circular. 6km (4 miles),
typical time around 2 hours.
OS maps: 106 Landranger, Pathfinder 685 & 686, (SE 63/73 & SE 83/93).
Points of interest: Bubwith is an interesting village with its ancient crossing of the River Derwent. All the route is good for nature lovers with many wild flowers and bird life, nature site at Dingle Dell. Several good pubs quite close to the trail, shops in Bubwith and Holme-on-Spalding-Moor.
Tourist information office: nearest office is at Selby.
Tel: (01757) 703263.
Cycling: This is a 'permissive bridleway', as such you can use your bike along all but the first 1km at Dingle Dell, subject to any notices issued by the council. The western end can become rather overgrown in summer months. By using the country lanes to the north of the trek, you can make your cycle route circular, returning to Bubwith via Everingham, Seaton Ross, Laytham and Aughton Common on the B1228.

If you are looking for a dramatic trek with spectacular views, then Bubwith Rail Trail is not the one. However, the walk is easy going and relaxing and offers peace and tranquillity surrounded by an abundance of wildlife and nature. Against the backdrop of our railway heritage most will enjoy this untaxing walk from the River Derwent to the edge of the Wolds.

Walk 2: The Hudson Way from Market Weighton to Beverley.

With the previous walk located to the south west of Market Weighton, this second walk starts close to Market Weighton town centre and heads off to the east towards the busy town of Beverley. As explained in walk one, this old railway route once formed part of the former Hull - Beverley - Market Weighton - York line. It also closed in the mid sixties under the Beeching plan, but unlike the Selby to Market Weighton and Driffield route, this line was actually said to be making a profit at the time of closure. Perhaps with further investment the line should have had a more certain future. Sadly it was swept away and left many of the local population without an important means of transport. On the other hand, closure once again brought a tranquil peace to this particularly attractive part of the Yorkshire Wolds.

The railway was constructed with two tracks and thus has a wide trackbed. Unlike the Bubwith Trail, it has far more earthworks which form the route as it climbs over the chalk hills, then down towards Beverley, connecting at a former junction on the Hull to Scarborough railway line about 2km north of the town.

I have again described the route from west (Market Weighton) to east (Beverley) and as with the last walk, you have many options where you can join or leave the trail.

The town of Market Weighton is a pleasant start or finish to a ramble. It has a few shops, public houses and amenities along with places to park your car. The main A1079 trunk road from York to Hull bypasses the town to the south, with the A614 several kilometres to the north and west. Although the main station site has been enveloped with new buildings, you only have to go a short way to pick up the line of the old railway tracks heading to Driffield and Beverley.

The Driffield line strikes out to the north east on an embankment, whilst the Hudson Way to Beverley continues straight on to the east in a shallow cutting. This first section of the walk is used by the long distance footpath - The Wolds Way. This 127km footpath (79 miles) covers the entire length of the Yorkshire Wolds from Hessle in the south to Filey Brigg, just north of Flamborough Head on the coast.

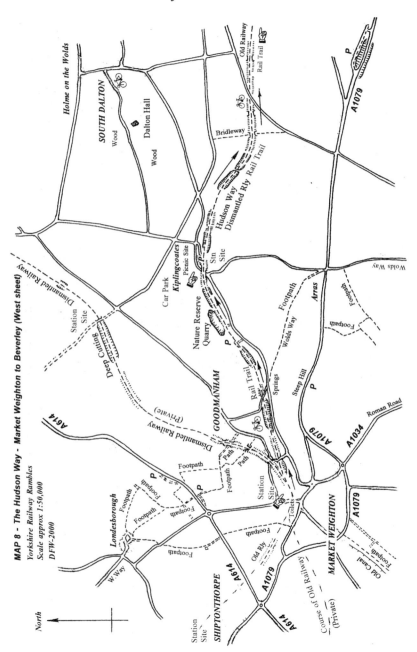

MAP 8 - The Hudson Way - Market Weighton to Beverley (West sheet)
Yorkshire Railway Rambles
Scale approx 1:50,000
DFW-2000

Around the Heart of The Wolds

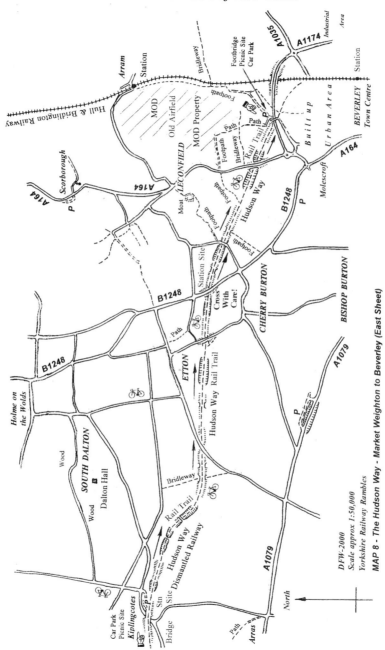

DFW-2000
Scale approx 1:50,000
Yorkshire Railway Rambles
MAP 8 - The Hudson Way - Market Weighton to Beverley (East Sheet)

At this point you are less than a kilometre from Market Weighton but already you are onto the Wolds hills. With the small village of Goodmanham due north, the railway slips into a shallow cutting with thick undergrowth to the south side.

Many fresh water springs emerge from the ground over the next kilometre before the scenery changes to the familiar dry valleys that are typical of porous chalk hills. Although a narrow lane runs parallel to the railway for 6km, this is a very tranquil area and very rich in wildlife. 4km from Market Weighton a former chalk quarry is passed located on the north side of the line. This is now designated as an official nature reserve with information boards at the entrance. Access is open to the public but the marked paths should be followed at all times and dogs are not allowed.

Continuing east a fine single arch brick bridge is crossed and Kiplingcoates railway station site is located ahead. This has been pleasantly redeveloped with further car parking and picnic facilities and a cafe located in the former station buildings.

This handsome station is in a very rural setting with no apparent village to serve. You have to look back into the history of the construction of the line to appreciate the curious logic of this. This area is part of the vast estate of Lord Hotham and when it came to crossing the land by railway, stations had to be located where he gave permission. Hence no station served the village of Etton, whilst his Lordship had the almost exclusive use of Kiplingcoates station 3km west of his residence at Dalton Hall. It was again at his Lordship's insistence that this line never had any train services on a Sunday, this lasted throughout its entire one hundred year history.

Continuing east from the station you have a succession of shallow cuttings and embankments with the occasional occupation bridge to give access to the many farms along the route. The hamlet of Gardham is passed to the south, whilst to the north, the elegant 60 metre high spire of St Mary's church at South Dalton village can be seen 2kms away. 5kms after Kiplingcoates station the village of Etton lies less than 1km north of the route of the line. A derelict windmill stands close to the access of a minor road between Cherry Burton and Etton. Here you have the option of a short detour to the refreshments served at one or other of the public houses in either village.

Further to the east the intensely farmed land is less hilly as the chalk ground slowly gives way to clay. After another short cutting the

Kiplingcoates Station and train c.1940s

busy B1248 Beverley to Malton road needs to be crossed with care. This is the only main road you need to cross at the same level on the entire walk and, following the removal of the railway bridge soon after the closure of the line, ramps where installed giving access for everyone including cycles and wheelchairs.

The site of Cherry Burton station is passed next on the route. This station is another one illogically placed some distance away from the village it serves. The railway promoters wanted to build this station on the road between Etton and Cherry Burton where it would have served the needs of both communities much more comprehensively. A commercial transport company now operates from the old station yard at the south side of this line.

Another kilometre east and the line is close to a number of historical sites. 1km north, by the village of Leconfield, is the site of a castle bearing the same name. Once a stronghold of the powerful Percy family, this substantial manor house surrounded by a moat was razed to the ground around 1608. Many of the interior fittings were removed to another Percy stronghold, the castle at Wressle, with other items going to Kilnwick Hall 7km to the north.

Between the castle and the railway is the site of the village of Raventhorpe, one of the hundreds of 'lost' villages in the East Riding. South of the line is the site of a moated farm known as Parkhouse. Footpaths are marked that will lead you past the site of the castle but be aware not stray onto private farmland. In the last few hundred metres of the walk you cross under the Beverley - Driffield road where to the north is the large site of Leconfield airfield. It is still home to helicopters of the RAF Air Sea Rescue service, though its main use today is as an armed forces agency driver training school.

The north eastern Beverley bypass is now ahead and a well placed car park and picnic area is located at the north side of the road. You can terminate the walk here or continue south across the footbridge and onto the town centre 1.5km due south.

Beverley is a buoyant historical town with a lively market square and an excellent array of shops, public houses and restaurants. Most notable amongst the historic buildings are St Mary's Church and Beverley Minster, both well worth visiting, as are many other buildings in the centre of the town. The nearby Beverley Museum of Army Transport contains some excellent exhibits including railway locomotives and rolling stock of both standard and narrow gauge.

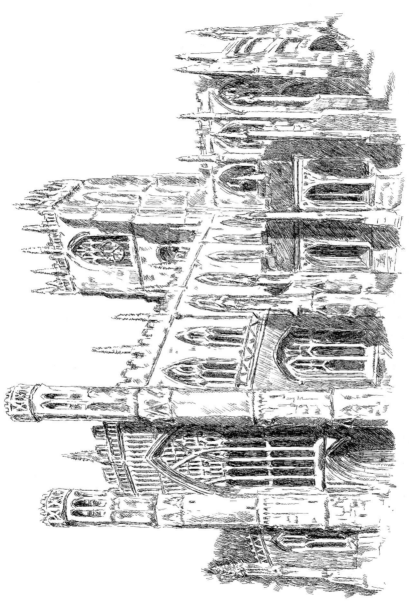

St Marys Church Beverley

Fact File -The Hudson Way

Start/Finish: Market Weighton to the north side of Beverley.
Grid Refs: SE 878420 & TA 028414
A very scenic trek with only one major road crossing, (B1248 at Cherry Burton).
Location: Market Weighton town centre to picnic site on the north eastern bypass 1.5km north of Beverley town centre, (A1174).
Max. length of walk: 16km (10 miles), typical walking time is about 4 hours, one way.
Length of shorter walk: 6km (4 miles) to Kiplingcoates car park, typical time 2 hours, one way. Many options from access points.
OS maps: 106 Landranger, Pathfinder 675 & 676, (SE 84/85 & TA 04/14).
Points of interest: An abundance of wildlife with nature reserve at Kiplingcoates old quarry, beautiful Wolds scenery. Good village pubs at Etton, Cherry Burton and South Dalton, tea room open at Kiplingcoates in summer.
Tourist information office: Beverley. Tel: (01482) 876430.
Cycling: This is another 'permissive bridleway' so subject to no variation notices by the council, the complete length can be cycled. Plenty of quiet lanes run east/west along the old railway tracks, so you can make your route circular by taking your return journey through Etton, South Dalton and Goodmanham back to the start. No bikes or pets in the nature reserve please.

Not all railway walks are lengthy trails covering most of the route of the former tracks. Indeed many short sections have become adopted as footpaths having been used by locals as short cuts or by dog walkers trying to get away from the traffic. The next trek falls into this category, and is set against a rich bed of history on the boundary of East and North Yorkshire.

Walk 3: A Ramble Over Stamford Bridge Viaduct.

We are again on the former York to Hull railway route, this time just 10km east, north east of York, at the small town of Stamford Bridge. Our history books tell us of the significance of this location almost a thousand years ago. In 1066 a famous battle raged close to the town and ensured that we do not speak Norwegian (a blessing if you have ever struggled with the basics of this language!). King Harold defeated the invaders from Scandinavia just months before heading south with his army to take on William the Conqueror at Hastings. Further information about the battle can be gleaned from display boards located around the village centre.

Stamford Bridge is located on the A166 with its famous narrow stone road bridge crossing the waters of the River Derwent. The road links York with Driffield and Bridlington climbing the Wolds escarpment at Garrowby Hill. Most of the town is situated on the east side of the river in the East Riding of Yorkshire. Over the river to the west you are in the county of North Yorkshire and a short journey to the A64 trunk road around the city of York.

Just by the stone road bridge is a well signposted car park and picnic site off the main road, with shops, public houses and toilets all close by.

The very imposing railway viaduct dominates the view to the south. Until recently this magnificent bridge had an uncertain future. The most substantial structure on the Hull to York railway, it had fallen into decay since the closure of the railway in November 1965. Originally opened in October 1847 it had ten masonry arches at the east end and five at the west end and had a main girder span of approximately 40 metres over the river. Although a listed structure, the cost of making it safe had clouded the future of the viaduct for many years. Finally agreement was reached to spend a significant sum of money repairing it and developing a short walkway over the bridge from the former station site. Having left your transport near to the road bridge, walk down stream at the east side of the river Derwent towards the viaduct. As described earlier, the Derwent is notorious for flooding and at such times the picnic area and car park will be lost under the flood waters rushing south to the Ouse and Humber.

The viaduct is only a few hundred metres to the south with a footpath along both banks of the river. View the structure in detail from the underside and ponder how many bricks make up the fine masonry arches. The main span now gleams with six shallow arched girders spanning the river below.

To walk across the structure head east past the arches and to the north side of the embankment. The path slowly rises up to former rail

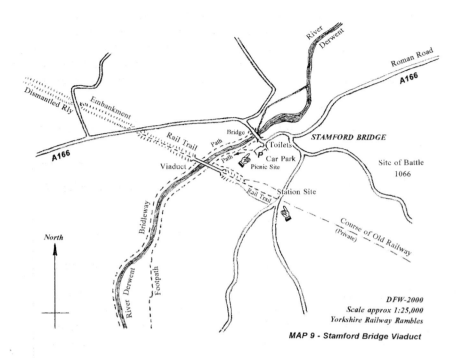

MAP 9 - Stamford Bridge Viaduct

DFW-2000
Scale approx 1:25,000
Yorkshire Railway Rambles

level where a few further steps brings you into the site of the former goods sidings. The station site itself is a few hundred metres further east and includes the original three bay engine and goods shed which is still in good repair having been refurbished and extended. The platforms and the goods loading bay are all still in situ too, and even a level crossing gate, once a familiar railway sight, stands at the far end of the station by Church Road. Turning back to walk westward we can now stroll over the viaduct. The parapets have been repaired along with a close iron fence over the centre span, so you do not need to worry unduly about the safety of children or dogs. A good view is afforded back to the stone arched road bridge to the north, while to the south the river is soon lost from view as it meanders over the flat Vale of York. You can continue along the railway embankment to the A166 road crossing, although with the old bridge removed several years ago you have to scramble down to the road level. The embankment continues another few hundred metres before again coming to another former bridge site over a country lane.

Wild young trees and bushes have established themselves along the embankment making it a haven for wildlife and with so much water about there are always plenty of birds to view together with swans and ducks squabbling around on the river banks. You can head back over the viaduct and down to the car park, or take a circular route by crossing the pedestrian bridge at the side of the stone road bridge (see map). For a pleasant few hours strolling through this historical part of our countryside, Stamford Bridge is an excellent place complete with several pubs and a picnic area.

Fact File - Stamford Bridge Viaduct Walk

Start/Finish: Stamford Bridge.
Grid Refs: SE 711555. A short historical ramble with some very fine views.
Location: Car park next to A166 road bridge in the centre of Stamford Bridge village.
Max. length of walk: 3km (2 miles), typical walking time 1 hour.
OS maps: Landranger 106, Pathfinder 665, (SE 65/75).
Points of interest: Site of battle in 1066, road bridge and railway viaduct over the River Derwent. Shops, public houses and all amenities available.
Tourist information office: York, Tel: (01904) 621756.
Cycling: Route over viaduct is not practical for bikes but many quiet lanes between Stamford Bridge and Pocklington make for a pleasant flat ride. Should you prefer a more hilly route keep going east towards the Wolds between Garrowby and Warter.

Before leaving these two key railway routes which made Market Weighton an important and busy junction station, mention should be made of a short section of the Market Weighton - Driffield route that may also soon be given over to nature and ramblers at Middleton-on-the-Wolds. This small village mid-way between Market Weighton and Driffield is choked by the A614 trunk road running through its centre. For many years the line of the railway which ran just to the north of the village centre was protected from development after closure. It was intended that it could form the route of a much needed bypass for the village. However current thinking is to build a completely new road further north still and to bypass both Middleton-on-the-Wolds and Bainton. If this occurs it will leave the thickly wooded embankments available for a short walk from the site of the old station, (grid reference SE 944498), westward to the former bridge that carried the main road over the railway. It is hoped that the status of this short section will be confirmed in the not too distant future.

Walk 4: Around the Lost Village of Wharram Percy.

Our last look at old railway trails in the Heart of the Wolds takes us onto the high chalk hills and a brief walk just over the border into North Yorkshire.

The picturesque setting of the Driffield and Malton Railway is covered in my last book 'Yorkshire Wolds Wanderings' and, like the Hull and Barnsley Railway, was closed well before Dr. Beeching arrived on the scene. This particular diminutive railway was opened in 1853 with the grand idea to provide a shorter route between the ports of Hull and Newcastle. It would connect up with another new stretch of railway between Malton and Thirsk and thus bypass York. It never even came close to fulfilling its vision and the line remained as a sleepy rural backwater threading its way over and through some of the finest landscape in the Yorkshire Wolds.

It was not an easy line to construct. Much of the route laboured over and through the chalk hills with the tunnel at Burdale particularly difficult for the little company to overcome. The original plans for a twin track railway with no tight curves or steep gradients quickly degenerated into a single track railway twisting and winding along the valley floor to keep the costs down.

With the early closure to passengers in 1950, then goods traffic in 1958, much of the trackbed was quickly lost and reverted back to farming. One short section of the trackbed to the north of Burdale tunnel has become the route of an overgrown footpath that originally ran along the side of the line from Wharram station to the site of Wharram Percy village. This is the most outstanding of all the 'lost village' sites in the north east of England. Forty years of excavation has revealed a wealth of fascinating information about this medieval settlement tracing its history back over the last thousand years.

The footpath, it is not a bridleway, can be accessed from the B1248 Malton to Beverley road using the lane to the south of Wharram-le-

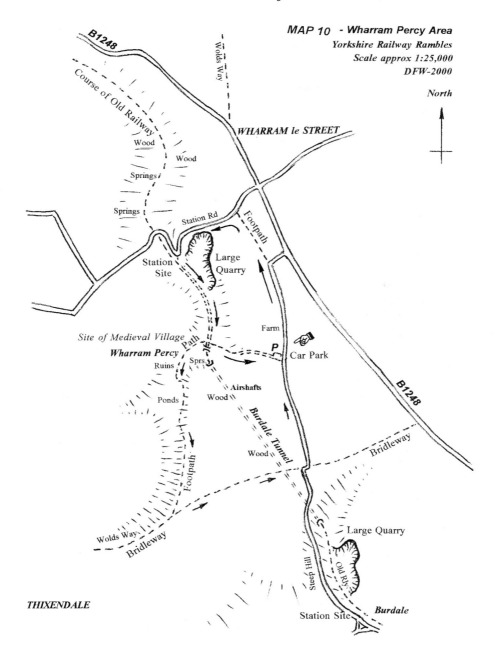

MAP 10 - Wharram Percy Area
Yorkshire Railway Rambles
Scale approx 1:25,000
DFW-2000

North

street. A car park is provided close to Bella Farm. Although only a few kilometres of this circular walk is along the railway, the setting is excellent and gives you so many options to enjoy the Wolds' dales with so much history at your feet.

To cover the walk in an anti-clockwise direction, leave the car park by the minor road and walk northwards. Where the road turns sharp right, take the footpath straight on until you reach Station Road. Go to the left down the steep hill to the station site and turn left along the old railway track.

The buildings of what was once Wharram station still remain and are now a private residence. Walk south along the trackbed and into the overgrown valley of this beautiful dale.

The substantial chalk quarry to your left is one of several that provided a number of trains each day to help retain the line after the closure to passengers. The excavated material was taken north via the Malton and Thirsk railway for use in the blast furnaces of Teeside. All the quarries including the massive site at Burdale are now unworked. Many of the old buildings associated with the quarry workings still remain to the east of the old railway, but be advised to give them a wide berth as they are in a very dilapidated and possibly dangerous state.

The undergrowth has taken over the track side as you head south. A bubbling fresh water stream rushes northwards, first at the right side of the trackbed, then crossing under to the left. After a kilometre a dilapidated bridge crosses over the line with a footpath leading away to both your left and right immediately before this bridge. Beyond this bridge, but well hidden by the undergrowth, is the northern portal of Burdale tunnel (just over a kilometre long). The footpath to your right (west) will lead you to the medieval village site of Wharram Percy and, if you feel energetic, a longer trek over the hills to Thixendale. This now forms part of the re-routed Wolds Way long distance footpath from Hessle to Filey Brigg.

To return to the car park take the path to your left (east), over the stream and up the track for a ten minute walk back to your transport.

The area has many bridleways and quiet country lanes. If you want a good cycle route study the OS maps for this area for some great muscle tingling hills.

The line of the abandoned railway can still be clearly seen from the former Sledmere and Fimber station site further south, and up at

Leaving Burdale Tunnel c.1950s

both Settrington and North Grimston further North. The station site at Sledmere on the B1248 and B1251 is now a pleasant picnic area with public toilets and a snack kiosk, although little evidence of the station itself now remains.

Fact File - The Wharram Percy Walk

Start/Finish: Car park near Bella Farm.
Grid Refs: SE 867644. A short circular walk with a few hills.
Location: Just off B1248 near Wharram-le-Street village, (signpost to Burdale).
Length of walk: 4km (3 miles), typical walking time about one hour, circular.
Length of longer walk: 12km (8 miles), typical time 3 hours, circular including Wharram Percy and Deep Dale.
OS maps: Landranger 100 & 101, Pathfinder 656, (SE 86/96).
Points of interest: Deserted medieval village and church at Wharram Percy. Picnic site with toilets, 5km south east on B1248 Fimber Station site.
Tourist information office: Malton, Tel: (01653) 600048.
Cycling: This walk is not available to the cyclist. However the area provides a maze of circular routes using the very quiet lanes and bridleways. Look at the OS maps and get your leg muscles tingling on these excellent Wolds hills!

Chapter 5

Tracing Hull and Barnsley Tracks

In this chapter we take a look at three short walks that are all within easy striking distance of the city of Hull and ideal for a leisurely Sunday afternoon stroll.

Without a doubt, the most difficult railway to be constructed in the East Riding of Yorkshire was the Hull, Barnsley and West Riding Junction Railway and Dock Company of 1885. This late arrival to the area, built to try and break the monopoly of the North Eastern Railway company, had to contend with numerous topographical problems which it encountered in this locality.

With all suitable level land already taken by the NER, the Hull and Barnsley Railway (as it was always known), had to build up, over and through the obstructing hills of the southern Wolds. Steep gradients, three tunnels (the longest was Drewton at almost 2km in length) and mile after mile of deep cuttings and embankments. Not only did this make the Hull and Barnsley a very costly railway to construct, but it was also an expensive line to operate as heavy coal trains always struggled to climb over the gradients.

The route was undoubtedly well constructed, but at a price that was to always restrict its ability to compete effectively with the dominant NER. So much so that this beautiful scenic line finally succumbed and was absorbed by the NER just prior to the grouping of the railway companies in 1922. With the birth of the London and North Eastern Railway and the difficult operation of the H&B route, traffic was steadily diverted to run along the level tracks of the former NER along the north bank of the Humber.

With only a small passenger service, the H&B soon became a target for possible closure. The line was steadily cut back to Howden, then Little Weighton and finally to Springhead, just to the west of Hull, in 1964.

A small section of the original line is still open and forms the present high level route around the city of Hull enabling access to the eastern docks. Ironically this enabled the removal of the ground level routes of the former NER which had strangled the city with multiple level crossings for many years. Another short section of the former H&B main line is also used to give access to the 'merry-go-round' trains delivering coal to Drax Power Station near Carlton Towers.

In view of the early closure of much of this railway, most of the land was sold off as long as forty years ago for development, or to the local farmers. One 5km section to the north of Gilberdyke and Newport was lost forever under the of the M62 trans Pennine motorway. However, three short sections have survived to be adopted as footpaths at Eastrington, Weedley Springs near South Cave and at Willerby.

Walk 5. The Eastrington Nature Ramble

This pleasant little walk near Eastrington starts from a small car park 1km west of the village and 4km east, north east from Howden, just off the B1230. It is linked to a nature reserve which is formed from a number of ponds in this locality. The original pits were created when clay was extracted from the land for the manufacture of tiles and bricks. The pits subsequently flooded leaving the ponds which have gradually been taken back by nature. It also is possible that earth

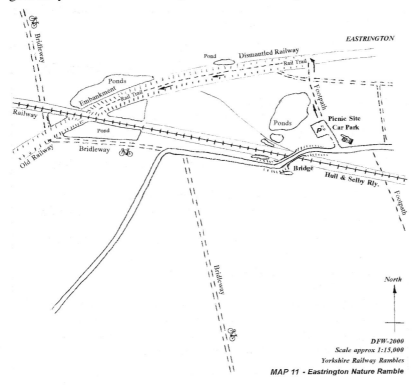

DFW-2000
Scale approx 1:15,000
Yorkshire Railway Rambles
MAP 11 - Eastrington Nature Ramble

from these ponds may also have been used by the railway builders to form the embankments that once took the H&B lines over the ground level North Eastern tracks.

The car park is on the left of the road just a few metres from the overbridge which crosses the present Leeds - Hull railway lines. Leaving your transport, you can meander around the ponds absorbing the peace and tranquillity before walking a short distance to the trackbed of the H&B. At this point turn west (left) and make your way just under a kilometre along the steadily rising embankment. The bridge that once carried the H&B tracks over the NER tracks was dismantled many years ago, so the walk terminates at this point immediately in front of a steep slope down to the Leeds - Hull railway lines below.

The undergrowth on the sides of the embankment is very thick and gives good cover for the many birds, animals and insects in this marshy area. Just to the south of the Leeds - Hull tracks, a bridleway can provide the start of a 7 to 8km circular walk or cycle ride, taking in the villages of Portington and Eastrington.

Fact File - Eastrington Nature Ramble

Start/Finish: Eastrington picnic site.
Grid Refs: SE 787298. A short nature ramble.
Location: 2km north of B1230, (old A63), 1km west of Eastrington village.
Max. length of walk: 2km (1.5 miles), typical walking time 1 hour.
Length of longer walk: 6km (4 miles), typical time 2 hours.
OS maps: Landranger 106, Pathfinder 685 & 694, (SE 63/73 & SE 62/72).
Points of interest: Nature site with ponds, so wildlife in abundance. Shop and public house in Eastrington village.
Tourist information office: Humber Bridge,
Tel: (01482) 640852.
Cycling: The nature ramble is on footpaths only but you can make a circular cycle route of around 8km, plus by setting off along the bridleway south of the Hull to Leeds railway, taking in the villages of Portington and Eastrington.

Walk 6. Weedley Springs and Drewton Dale

The Wolds hills to the east of South Cave are excellent walking country and I described many circular routes for this area in my previous book, 'Yorkshire Wolds Wanderings'. Though only a few kilometres from the busy A63/M62, the peace and tranquillity of this part of the Wolds is very special. The walk down to the trackbed at Weedley Springs can be accessed from the B1230 Walkington to North Cave Road or from the Beverley Road from South Cave to Little Weighton and Willerby.

If sensibly parked, cars can be left just off Beverley Road 1km from the village (though please take care not to block gateways). The bridleway heading due west is well used. 1km from the road a footpath leads down to Weedley Springs to the north.

A short distance before the trackbed a bridleway crosses from left to right. To the west this takes you to Drewton Dale, to the east are the fresh water springs, then down to the railway.

The steep cliff down to the springs was actually created by the railway navvies building the railway in the early 1880s. It was not intended to create a tunnel at this location, but the problems encountered whilst building a main line railway over the springs necessitated changing the route to the north and building Weedley Tunnel on a slight curve through the hillside.

Walking past the springs to the east will bring you to the railway trackbed. Although a bridleway, high styles, complete with barbed wire, make this unsuitable for cyclists. Once on the trackbed the next kilometre gives you a splendid walk east along this valley towards Sugar Loaf Tunnel, with the 2km long Drewton Tunnel beyond.

This area of the Wolds demonstrates the difficulties in building this railway and why it was so much more expensive than the North Eastern route to the south. The chalk cuttings are vast and whilst the rock was hard to cut through, equally it could become unstable once disturbed. Thus costly retaining walls were often required and heavy maintenance costs in clearing the chalk falls. Occupation bridges were common, giving access for local farmers. The gradients were severe for a main line railway and meant heavy coal trains had to be 'double-headed' with two locomotives, or split into two shorter sections and run over the summit separately. Now a haven for wildlife, the line is a silent but awe inspiring monument to our Victorian railway engineers.

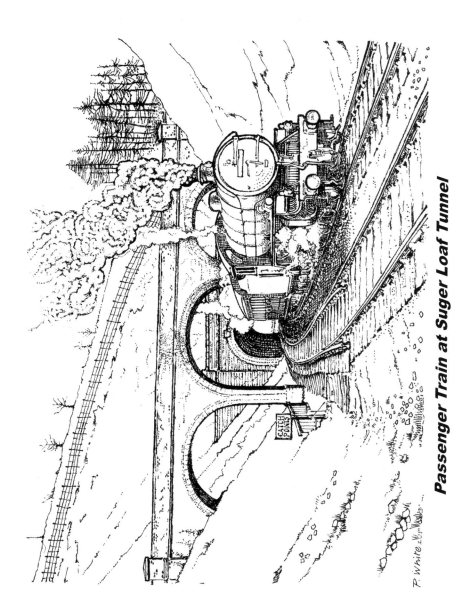

Passenger Train at Suger Loaf Tunnel

P. White

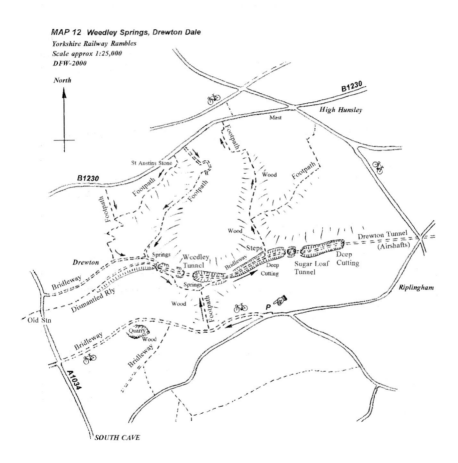

MAP 12 Weedley Springs, Drewton Dale
Yorkshire Railway Rambles
Scale approx 1:25,000
DFW-2000

Before you reach the first tunnel, the path heads to your left (north) up a very steep set of steps to the top of the cutting and through a thickly wooded dale. If you wish to make your walk circular, you can ascend this dale up to the B1230, 1.5km north of the railway, then south east back down to Drewton Dale and the area around Weedley Tunnel. An exhilarating walk at any time of the year with a kilometre of steady climbing, followed by a long decent.

Be aware that all the tunnels are unsafe and located on private land and must not be ventured into. The many footpaths and bridleways are however well sign posted. This is a splendid part of the Wolds and always good for spending a few hours walking.

Fact File - The Weedley Springs Ramble

Start/Finish: Beverley Clump.
Grid Refs: SE 945328. Very attractive hilly area of the Wolds.
Location: South Cave to Beverley road, 3km north east of South Cave village.
Max. length of walk: 4km (2.5 miles),
typical walking time 1 hour.
Length of longer walk: 7km (5 miles), typical time 2 hours.
OS maps: Landranger 105, Pathfinder 686, (SE 83/93).
Points of interest: Weedley Springs between two old tunnels, refreshments available in South Cave village.
Tourist information office: Humber Bridge,
Tel: (01482) 640852.
Cycling: The link from the chalky lane to the railway is a footpath only, but there are plenty of options for a hilly circular route taking in Low Drewton, North Cave, Hotham, South Newbald, High Hunsley, Riplingham and back to the lay-by at the top of the hill at Beverley Clump.

Walk 7. The Springhead Trail

To the east of Willerby and Kirkella station, on the descent into Hull, the topography of the Hull and Barnsley route changed again, swapping deep chalk cuttings for high embankments created from the spoil removed from the hills. Other than the present overhead freight line around the city, only a few short sections of original trackbed now remain. These are to the west of Springhead with only the stretch from Willerby to the King George V playing fields in Anlaby as a public footpath.

There is a large car park with public toilets just off Beverley Road in Willerby village. The original station and large goods yard was situated just to the north of this road on the line of the present bypass. Housing development has occurred over the last two decades and the old site has been lost forever. The car park itself is actually on part of the original alignment where an overbridge carried the railway across to the east.

A flight of steps created at the eastern end of the car park take you up onto the short remaining section of thickly wooded embankment. It continues east for almost a kilometre to Gorton Road. The embankment to the east of the Gorton Road has been removed along with the site of Forty Steps. This was a local name given to the wooden steps that once crossed over the line, taking the footpath onto Wolfreton Road and the original Springhead Inn. The memory of the place is however preserved in a local residential street name.

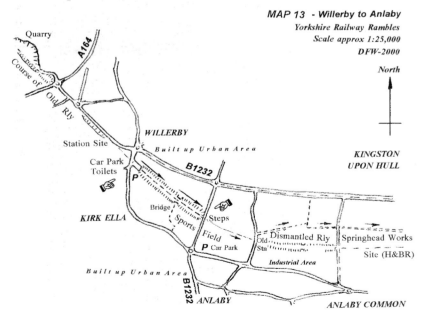

MAP 13 - Willerby to Anlaby
Yorkshire Railway Rambles
Scale approx 1:25,000
DFW-2000

North

KINGSTON UPON HULL

Willerby and Kirkella Station c.1930s

P.White

You can continue to walk eastward on the new path past the houses and across Wolfreton Road. A further track continues to the old waterworks pumping station at Springhead which until recently was home to a small museum.

Just beyond this location were the extensive railway workshops known as Springhead Works. These were the main maintenance and repair shops of the Hull and Barnsley company. There were also extensive coal sidings at the site which covered an area of several square kilometres, stretching from Springhead Lane to Calvert Lane. The works survived as a wagon repair shop until 1971, but after closure all evidence of the site disappeared under modern housing developments. A wide bridleway still exists which can take you through the residential area all the way to the Priory roundabout at the junction of Spring Bank West and Calvert Lane.

From here a bus can return you to Willerby and back to the start of this walk.

Fact File - The Springhead Trail

Start/Finish: Willerby car park.
Grid Refs: SE 026300. A short elevated walk, can be extended to Priory roundabout through residential area.
Location: Just south of Willerby Square, B1232 (old A164).
Max. length of walk: 2km (1.5 miles),
typical walking time 1 hour.
OS maps: Landranger 106, Pathfinder 695, (SE 82/92).
Points of interest: Overgrown chalk embankment giving vantage view point. Springhead Waterworks building.
Tourist information office: Humber Bridge,
Tel: (01482) 640852.
Cycling: This is an urban area and the route is not entirely suitable for cycles. There are better cycle routes available further to the west and back into the countryside.

Chapter 6

The Lost Railways of Holderness

Walk 8. The South Holderness Rail Trail.

The Hull and Holderness Railway was a local company established to link the town of Hull with the east coast in the middle of the eighteenth century. The original plans were equally enthusiastic about terminating the line at either Easington or the tiny village of Withernsea. The route finally adopted was built and opened in June 1853. It began with a new station near Victoria Dock on Hedon Road in Hull and ran on to Hedon and Patrington with a terminus at Withernsea.

Although the line proved popular when it opened, it was not long before financial difficulties forced a sale to the North Eastern Railway company in 1862. The NER soon had trains running to its new Hull terminus at Paragon Station via a route which encircled the town on a ground level branch built to gain access to Victoria Dock.

Much of the line had been constructed as single track, but over the years all but two sections were doubled to cope with increasing holiday and commuter traffic. Indeed this railway line enjoyed a healthy level of both passenger and goods trade for most of its existence. Both commuters and holiday makers used the line regularly, with many people from the Hull area making day trips to enjoy the sea air, or even just for an evening dance at the Grand Pavilion in Withernsea.

Road haulage did take much of the goods traffic away in the last decade of the railway, but passenger traffic was still quite healthy when the Beeching report recommended the coast lines from Hull to Hornsea and Hull to Withernsea for closure. Within a few short years of closure the extensive development of the offshore natural gas fields and land terminals just down the coast at Easington began. Had the original 1850s plan to terminate the railway at Easington been adopted then with the vast amount of construction traffic on offer, the fate of the line may have been different.

That is possibly the author indulging in some wishful thinking! Though had the railway been operated efficiently, perhaps it could have been profitable as a commuter line and today people may well have preferred to travel to work by train instead of enduring a frustrating hour sat in traffic queues on Hedon or Holderness Road every week day.

Yorkshire Railway Rambles 1. North and East

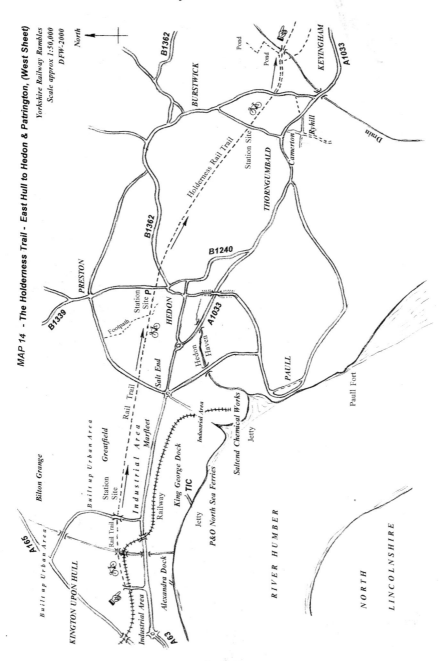

MAP 14 - The Holderness Trail - East Hull to Hedon & Patrington, (West Sheet)

Yorkshire Railway Rambles
Scale approx 1:50,000
DFW-2000

North

BURSTWICK

B1362

KEYINGHAM

A1033

Pond

Pond

Pond

Ryhill

Cameron

Drain

Station Site

THORNGUMBALD

Holderness Rail Trail

B1362

B1240

PRESTON

Station Site P

Footpath

B1339

HEDON

A1033

Hedon Haven

PAULL

Paull Fort

Salt End

Rail Trail

Bilton Grange

Built up Urban Area

Built up Urban Area

Greatfield

Station Site

Rail Trail

Industrial Area

Marfleet

Railway

King George Dock

TIC

Industrial Area

Saltend Chemical Works

Jetty

Jetty

A165

Rail Trail

KINGTON UPON HULL

Built up Urban Area

Industrial Area

Alexandra Dock

A63

Jetty

P&O North Sea Ferries

RIVER HUMBER

NORTH

LINCOLNSHIRE

The Lost Railways of Holderness

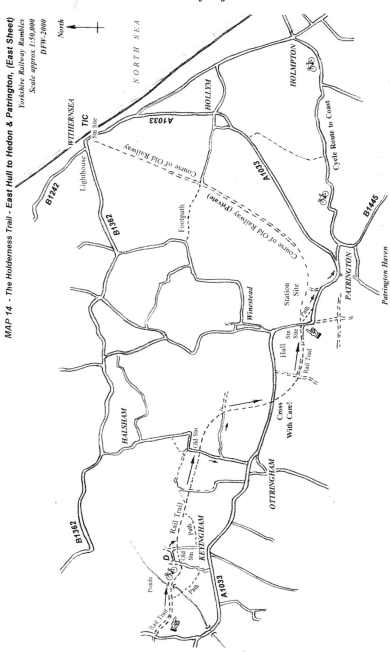

MAP 14 - The Holderness Trail - *East Hull to Hedon & Patrington, (East Sheet)*

Yorkshire Railway Rambles

Scale approx 1:50,000

DFW-2000

North

NORTH SEA

WITHERNSEA

TIC

Stn Site

Lighthouse

B1242

B1362

A1033

HOLLYM

HOLMPTON

Cycle Route to Coast

A1033

B1445

Footpath

Course of Old Railway

Course of Old Railway (Private)

Winestead

Station Site

PATRINGTON

Patrington Haven

Path

Stn Site

Hall

Rail Trail

Cross With Care!

HALSHAM

Old Stn

OTTRINGHAM

B1362

Rail Trail

Old Stn

Path

KEYINGHAM

Path

D

Ponds

Rail Trail

A1033

To the relief of motorists in the Hull area, the inner circle of ground level railway lines closed shortly after the branch lines to Withernsea and Hornsea had been lifted. All remaining rail traffic to the eastern docks and the BP Chemicals plant at Saltend was transferred to the high level outer circle built by the Hull and Barnsley Railway in the 1880s. The city instantly eliminated a host of level crossings that had been the bane of car drivers for many years and had even become embodied in the city's folklore.

A number of sections of old trackbed on the Withernsea branch were purchased by the County Council and recreation became the theme for the disused route. With the plain of Holderness predominately flat, the old line does not posses many engineering features worthy of note. Just a succession of small bridges that were required to cross numerous land drains and, naturally, those ever familiar level crossings with their gates, signal boxes and crossing keeper's cottages.

With local councils keen to promote the use of bicycles, this route was made suitable for both walking and cycling. It can be commenced just under 2km east from the Hull city centre with various access points to the old line between Southcoates Lane and Marfleet Lane. You can also follow new cycle lanes from the city centre to Newbridge Road, then left along Belmont Street to the actual start of the trek at the end of Estcourt Street. The existing freight line runs just to the south of the rail trail as it makes its way to King George Dock and the BP Chemicals site at Saltend.

Inevitably, the first 4 to 5km of this trail pass through a very urban landscape, with the docks and many industrial premises occupying the land to the south. To the north side of the trail are the large housing estates of Preston Road and Greatfield. The former station at Marfleet is passed where, had history told a different story, the site could have been a busy commuter stop for thousands of local residents.

The surface of the trail is good for walking as you progress further east and leave the houses to recede into the distance. Industry is still dominant to the south though, with the vast chemical plant at Saltend dwarfing all other landmarks.

As you leave the eastern boundary of the city of Hull and cross the Saltend to Preston road, an area of land with a rather interesting history is passed. The fields between Hedon and Saltend played host to a racecourse which had two short spans of activity. Firstly from 1888 to 1895, followed by another brief spell of life for 8 years from 1901 until closure in 1909. In the 1930s the area saw use as Hull Municipal Airport, but this too failed with the outbreak of war and the proximity of the developing chemical plant.

The next 'chapter' was as a motorcycle speedway venue for Hull Angels speedway team. This existed for a few years after the war, but the potential crowds in Hull were a little too far distant to entice a healthy level of support.

When a racecourse, the site had its own halt built to handle the estimated 30,000 plus spectators that came to the first meetings. Today scant evidence remains of any of these ventures which have slipped quietly into oblivion.

Approaching the town of Hedon, the main settlement on the trail, a series of medieval ponds and earthworks are passed. These formed a twelfth century estate known as Twyers Hill just visible to the south of the line. The old station site has been converted into a smart residence with the long platform still visible despite thickets of brambles and young trees becoming established over the years. An area for parking is on the left just prior to the road crossing.

The old town centre of Hedon is just to the south side of the railway. The scene is dominated by the tower of St Augustine's Church. Locally known as the King of Holderness, this magnificent building was also started in the twelfth century with building work continuing over three

Ryehill Crossing c. 1930s

hundred years. Hedon's wealth and prosperity was significant throughout this period operating as a port through the nearby haven which connected with the Humber Estuary. Had it not been for the Humber's mud slowly silting-up the haven, the town may not have lost out to nearby Kingston upon Hull which systematically took away the shipping trade.

It is a ten minute detour into the town centre from the railway track where it crosses the B1240 road that links Hedon with the village of Preston.

As you leave the town of Hedon, the trackbed heads south east towards Keyingham. You cross the B1362 with houses to the south and open fields to the north. 3km to the north of the line is the village of Burstwick. The section from Hedon station to Burstwick remained single track throughout the history of the line. Like Hedon, Burstwick also has a rich history with a substantial castle existing at the north side of the village in the thirteenth and fourteenth century. It was abandoned by Sir Robert Constable when he built his family seat at Burton Constable Hall, 9km to the north, and took the title of the Lord of Holderness.

The station, which was officially named Ryehill and Burstwick, also served the villages of Thorngumbald, Camerton and Ryehill to the south of the line. Like most of the station buildings on the old line, it is now a private residence.

The following section from this station site to the next village of Keyingham is 3km long. Part of the route gives access to some ponds used for various other leisure pursuits and has become uneven due to vehicles eroding the surface. At Keyingham, the station buildings along with the complete station yard have all been sold off to a private purchaser, so the route around the site to the north side must be used. Turn left, then right to follow along the lane with a 'No through road' symbol. After a few hundred metres, turn right (south), then left again to get back onto the trail.

With much of the land to the south of Keyingham reclaimed from the marshy Humber flood plain, it is remarkable to think that three centuries ago, sailing ships could still navigate along the creek to the edge of the village. A 600m detour from the trail takes you south to the shops and public house on the main A1033 road.

Back along the trail and just over 2km east is the site of Ottringham station, this is actually over a kilometre to north of the village itself.

St Patrick's Church Patrington

The trail deteriorates significantly beyond this point on the route eastward to Winestead. A very small plaque advises you that you are still following a 'Permissive Bridleway' but it is a real challenge to try and use it as such since the next kilometre is heavily overgrown. If you are walking or cycling in shorts be prepared to pick up plenty of grazes and nettle stings as you push your way through the brambles and undergrowth. You may therefore wish to use the short detour south if you are cycling.

The trail now follows a long 'S' bend, going south to cross the A1033 road, then sweeping around to the east again. This is a particularly fast section of the A1033, so be aware and take care as you cross.

The next 2km of the trail beyond the road to the former Winestead station gives you a fine view of White Hall looking back to the north west. This area is quite wooded and provides shelter for the wildlife. The meagre use by passengers of Winestead station (Patrington station only a kilometre to the east was much larger) resulted in early closure to passenger trains in 1904. The signal box remained in use right up to the end of operations on the route, as it was used to control the level crossing and access to the single line. This section between Winestead and Ottringham being one of only two sections that remained as single track.

From this point on the rail trail, the old track bed has been sold off to the east of the A1033 road. You are only a kilometre from Patrington village to the south east. It is worth a visit if only to view the magnificent St Patrick's Church. A footpath cuts diagonally across the field opposite the point where you cross the road. The old station site is on your left as you enter the village with the Station Hotel still busy with passing trade. Along the broad main street through the village are a few shops and further public houses. The church with its 58 metre high spire is a thousand-year-old work of art. Known locally as the 'Queen of Holderness' this building, with its marvellous ornate stonework both inside and out, can absorb your interest for hours.

In the centre of the village the road to Withernsea sweeps round to the left while the B1445 to the right takes you to Easington, and beyond, to Kilnsea and Spurn Point.

It was the arrival of the railway that created the town of Withernsea which we know today. Sadly the old railway trail ends here, so to reach the town, you now need to catch a bus to travel the last 6km. If

Withernsea Lighthouse

you are on a cycle, you can take the minor lane due east to Holmpton, then either north to Withernsea or south to Easington. These routes are not the most direct, but will give you a pleasant end to a cycle ride to the coast.

The railway terminus in Withernsea was close to the sea front with the Station Hotel just to the south. In later years this building was purchased by the Reckitt family, a major employer with several factories in the city of Hull. Reckitts was a respected and conscientious firm who had a genuine concern for the welfare of its employees and used the building as a convalescent home.

The station site was razed in recent years and is now the home to a popular Sunday market which helps to keep visitors coming throughout the year. A full array of shops and public houses are available in the town, but the real historic gem is the gleaming white lighthouse. Built around 1894 and curiously set back 300 metres from the sea front, it was in use until the 1960s. It is now open to the public as a memorial museum to the actress Kay Kendall who had many local connections with the area. The long climb up the 127 steps to the old light platform will reward you with a breathtaking view of the landscape and sea for many, many miles around.

When compared with most of the rail trails detailed in this book, the Holderness route is a little disappointing. Although it is quite well maintained at the Hull end, the impression is that a lack of enthusiasm prevented its potential being properly realised to the east of the city. In addition to the obvious annoyance at finishing to the West of Patrington some 6km from the sea, the maintenance of the route is poor and the provisions to encourage its leisure use are almost nil. There is no proper provision for parking at any of the access points which means leaving cars on the road side, or in front of village houses, which is not ideal and something that most walkers do not like to do.

Further many parts of the trail are overgrown making access by cycle almost impossible. Few signs confirm the route, other than 'Private Property, No Entry', at several fences across the trail without even as much as an arrow to guide you around.

Nevertheless you can enjoy this trek and soak up a bit of the history of the surroundings as you do. There really is a lot of scope for the local authority to encourage greater use without infringing the rights and privacy of lineside residents.

Fact File - South Holderness Rail Trail.

Start/Finish: East Hull to Winestead.

Grid Refs: TA 123297 to TA 301234. A level trek from industrial East Hull across the Holderness plain.

Location: Belmont Street in East Hull to A1033 1km west of Patrington.

Max. length of walk: 21km (13 miles), typical walking time 5 hours, one way.

Length of shorter walk: 7km (5 miles), Hedon to Keyingham typical time 2 hours, one way.

OS maps: Landranger 106, Pathfinder 696 & 697, (TA 02/12 & TA 22/32).

Points of interest: The Churches in Hedon and Patrington in their very different ways are worthy of special note. Good array of shops, pubs and toilets in Hedon and Patrington. Some pleasant villages with pubs and shops not far from main route.

Tourist information office: Hull City Centre, Tel (01482) 223559, Withernsea, (seasonal office open during the summer months only), Tel: (01964) 615683.

Cycling: In theory you can use this 'permissive bridleway' throughout, but lack of proper maintenance means you will find it more difficult to cycle the route the further east you go. The advantage of being on a cycle is that you can extend your ride to the sea by using quiet lanes east of Patrington and Holmpton, then northward along the coast to Withernsea. Return via the B1362 through Halsham and Burstwick makes a pleasant circular route.

Walk 9 - The Hornsea Rail Trail.

The railway to Hornsea was opened eleven years after the Withernsea line in 1864. It too suffered the same fate and closed on the same day as its neighbour in October 1964. In many other ways it had a similar history; promoted by a local company and built as a single track railway, it also had to merge with the North Eastern Railway in 1866. The NER developed the line and doubled the tracks throughout its complete length. Again the promoters had hoped to build up a

MAP 15 - The Hornsea Trail - Hull to Hornsea, (South Sheet)

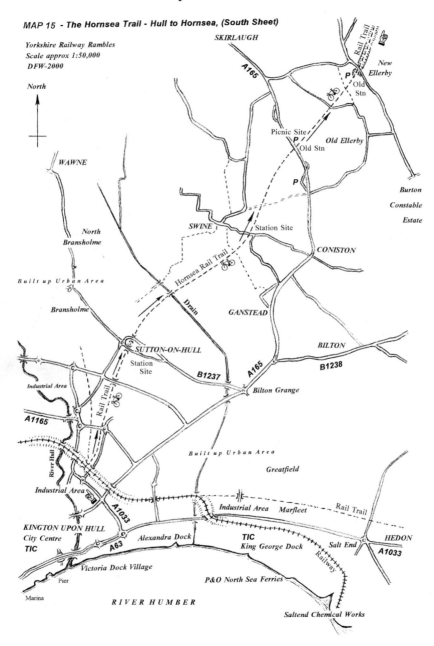

Yorkshire Railway Rambles
Scale approx 1:50,000
DFW-2000

North

SKIRLAUGH

Rail Trail

A165

New
Ellerby
Old
Stn

Picnic Site
Old Stn
Old Ellerby

WAWNE

P

Burton
Constable
Estate

North
Bransholme

SWINE
Station Site

CONISTON

Built up Urban Area

Hornsea Rail Trail

Bransholme

Drain

GANSTEAD

BILTON

SUTTON-ON-HULL
Station
Site

Rail Trail

B1237

A165

B1238

Industrial Area

Bilton Grange

A1165

Built up Urban Area

River Hull

Greatfield

Industrial Area

Rail Trail

A1033

Industrial Area   Marfleet

KINGTON UPON HULL
City Centre
TIC

A63

Alexandra Dock

TIC
King George Dock

Salt End

Railway

HEDON
A1033

Victoria Dock Village

Pier

P&O North Sea Ferries

Marina

RIVER HUMBER

Saltend Chemical Works

The Lost Railways of Holderness

MAP 15 - The Hornsea Trail - Hull to Hornsea, (North Sheet)

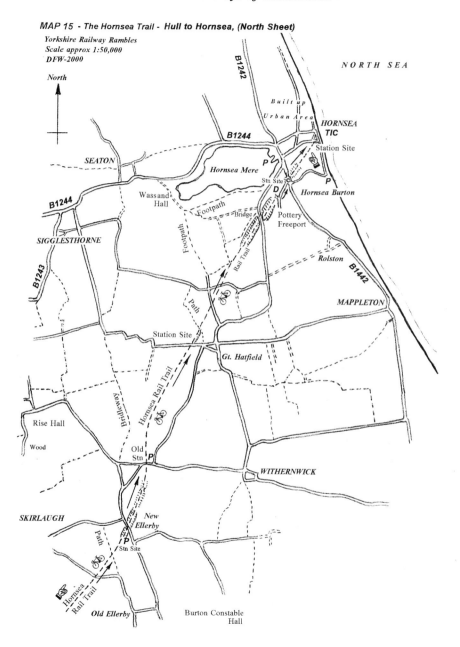

Yorkshire Railway Rambles
Scale approx 1:50,000
DFW-2000

North

NORTH SEA

B1242

Built up
Urban Area

HORNSEA
TIC

Station Site

B1244

P

Hornsea Mere

SEATON

Stn Site

P

D

Hornsea Burton

Wassand
Hall

Footpath

Bridge

Pottery
Freeport

B1244

Footpath

Rolston

B1442

SIGGLESTHORNE

B1243

Path

MAPPLETON

Station Site

Gt. Hatfield

Hornsea Rail Trail

Bridleway

Rise Hall

Wood

Old
Stn

P

WITHERNWICK

SKIRLAUGH

New
Ellerby

Path

P

Stn Site

Hornsea Rail Trail

Old Ellerby

Burton Constable
Hall

73

significant holiday trade and see the development of Hornsea as a major seaside resort.

Had only one of these two railways closed, it would have been interesting to see if the surviving one had gained any significant increase in holiday traffic to the coast. Clearly under the Beeching Plan the order was to cut back the system as savagely and as quickly as possible, British Railways were not looking for reasons to save lines and encourage more traffic. It seemed that the railways had become an unwanted transport system in the 1960s.

Running north, north east from the city of Hull, the line shared the ground level route out of Paragon station, passing Botanic Gardens station (formerly Cemetery Gates) at the junction of Spring Bank and Princes Avenue.

The former station site is now occupied by the new Old Zoological Public House and some of the original platform wall can still be seen in the car park. You can actually start the walk from this location, although a short diversion north along Princes Avenue, then right, to the end of Duesbery Street, is necessary before the original trackbed can be accessed. The city council have done a lot to preserve this route as a footpath and cycleway and although the first few kilometres from the Old Zoological pass through heavily industrialised areas, the route is nevertheless a surprising oasis in the heart of suburbia.

Once on the trackbed, the curved route of the original Victoria Dock Branch of 1853 continues around to Stepney station where the old platforms and station house are still extant. Beverley Road is then crossed and the route is straight on for about a half kilometre to the point where the Hull and Barnsley Railway branch to Cannon Street station crossed above. Remnants of the old embankment are still visible either side of the route. A new pedestrian bridge has been provided at this spot for crossing Barmston land drain.

On the right, beyond the trees, the Hull Municiple Charities Trusts' almshouses are passed, these were built in 1936. The old Sculcoates goods warehouse is still standing on the left, now ironically used by a road haulage firm. Next the River Hull is crossed via the 1907 NER swing bridge at Wincolmlee before entering the former Sculcoates station site just off Cleveland Street. In later years the North Eastern Railway relocated this station and it and the river crossing became known as Wilmington. Sadly, virtually all evidence of the railway at this point has been lost forever under industrial development, only the 1907

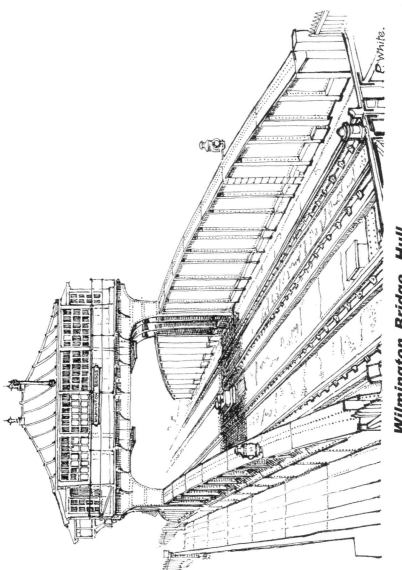

Wilmington Bridge, Hull

P. White.

ticket office built for Wilmington station still survives in Foster Street, in use as a workman's cafe.

This area of the city, being very industrial over the last century, employed thousands of people in a wide variety of factories and mills. A significant number of these sites have now been vacated as heavy industry and the manufacturing heart of our nation has increasingly moved to third world countries.

Immediately after crossing Cleveland street on an overbridge, the Withernsea line continued with the docks traffic to encircle the city. The Hornsea line branched to the north east and ran under the Hull and Barnsley high level railway route to Alexandra and King George Docks. The original alignment and the bridge itself cannot now be traced and in order to pick up the route a short diversion is required. Cross over Cleveland Street and head north for about 150m, pass under the overhead railway bridge, then turn left into Woodhall Street. Walking the full length of this road brings you to the site of the old Foredyke Stream. This wide land drain was filled in some years ago and now forms a cycle route and footpath from Witham, close to the city centre, northwards to Sutton Road. Turn south here and after about 50m you will be at the point where the stream was crossed by the old railway. This is an alternative starting point for the trek along the Hornsea Rail Trail and once on the trail you have a clear run from this dark area of the city, through 25km of Holderness countryside all the way to the North Sea at Hornsea.

The next kilometre takes you past Stoneferry on your left and the Summergangs area to your right. Right up to the crossing of Holderness Drain, some 7km to 8km north, the track has a tarmac surface and is in quite good order. If you are on your cycle take care passing the numerous barriers that prevent the use of motor bikes along the trail.

Shortly after traversing the old level crossing at Chamberlain Road the alignment of the former Stoneferry Goods Branch can be seen curving away to the left. It ran across the area now known as Sutton Fields Industrial Estate. This is a large expanse of modern factory units which provide a better environment for the thousands of people who travel each day to work in this part of the city.

After passing under the Sutton Road bridge the Bransholme housing estate, said to be the largest in Europe, is on your left and the village of Sutton on Hull is ahead of you. This village has a long history spanning nine hundred years.

You pass under the main street with the original bridge dated 1863 on the metal span, beyond which the railway station served the neighbourhood for a century. Since the closure of the line various schemes have been proposed to run trains into the city from here, but again, despite the tens of thousands of houses within walking distance, there was no will to reinstate logic into the local transport system!

The bypass constructed to the north side of Sutton village centre has enabled the area around the church to retain its rural charm. Refreshments are available at the shops and public houses along Church Street, the main thoroughfare.

Moving on, and the path follows through the underpass beneath the new road. There is much new housing hereabout, all built on land that was just green fields when the railway passed through. Soon however, the housing gives way to green fields and shortly, after the crossing of Holderness land drain, one of the many man made drains on the River Hull flood plain, a rather interesting area appears on your left.

Here, a number of ancient earthworks mark the site of a castle built around 1200 by Sir John Sahar.

The site is typical of the legion of ancient, abandoned castles and monasteries from this part of East Yorkshire where most visible signs of an actual building disappeared many centuries ago. Because building materials were so scarce in this marshy area, any neglected property was soon plundered and the stone and timber reused to build a farmhouse or barn. The earthwork remnants here are on private land so exploration beyond the public trail is not possible.

The surface of the trail is now the ash and cinders of the original railway trackbed but clear of any severe obstructions. 2km to the north east of the castle site is the location of the former station called Swine. The village of Swine, which it served, is the small community to the west of the trail, whilst to the east, is the larger village of Coniston on the A165 road. The station was originally called Coniston, but this was changed by the LNER, it is believed, to avoid confusion with Coniston in the Lake District.

That apart, there is much evidence here which indicates that the area has a rich and interesting history. It is believed that the Romans had a substantial camp nearby and various items have been unearthed dating from the fourth century. What is also known is that the village church was once a part of a Cistercian Priory founded in the mid-

Burton Constable Hall

twelfth century which survived until the reformation. To the west of the church are earthworks known as Giant's Hill, these are thought to have been the site of a motte type castle. There are a number of footpaths here which enable several short circular walks in this area.

2km further along the trail brings you to the busy A165 Hull to Bridlington road. After crossing this busy trunk road with great care, you will discover a small car park and picnic area. This has been created on the site of the former Skirlaugh station situated to the east side of the main road and which was actually over 2km south of the village it once served. With a further three stations built within the next few kilometres of the line, it is a little surprising that Skirlaugh station was ever built at all.

The next of these closely sited stations was at Old Ellerby, again a kilometre away from the small village and an early casualty of closure way back in 1902. The third station was at New Ellerby, which originally had the name 'Burton Constable' when first opened. The LNER changed it in early 1920s to avoid confusion with 'Constable Burton' station on the Hawes line in the Yorkshire Dales. Here a car park is provided at the south side of the road. The cutting beyond the road can become rather overgrown with nettles in the summer months but is still quite well drained.

This part of the trail from Skirlaugh to Whitedale is particularly attractive and is associated with a significant number of old country houses which adorn the area. These include Dowthorpe Hall, just north of the picnic site at Skirlaugh station, Wood Hall to the south of old Ellerby village and Ellerby Grange to the north, Langthorpe Hall to the west of New Ellerby station and the very grand Rise Hall to the west of Whitedale station.

It is quite possible that the land owners associated with these substantial houses dictated to the original promoters of the Hull and Hornsea Railway as to where stations must be sited. It would not be considered acceptable for the owners of such vast estates to have to share their station with their fellow gentleman neighbours in the mid nineteenth century!

The grandest and the most exclusive of all the houses in the Holderness area is Burton Constable Hall with its extensive parklands visible to the east of the railway route.

There is a public entrance to this property on the road to Sproatley about 3km south east of New Ellerby station. To include a visit to the

Hall on this walk would be quite a detour on foot but not beyond the capabilities of most determined walkers.

The Constable family have been the most notable and prominent landowners in Holderness for over eight centuries. As mentioned in the previous trek along the old Withernsea line, their original family home was near to Halsham not far north from the River Humber. Around 1570, the incumbent Sir John Constable made a significant start at moving the family seat to the location where Burton Constable Hall now stands. He enlarged an old tower house on the site and commenced many centuries of building and extending what eventually became this fine mansion within extensive parklands about 2km north of Sproatley village.

Like so many beautiful English country houses, the building slowly developed as different generations of the family added new extensions. However, parts of the original medieval tower house still remain in what is now the north wing.

Sir John, working with the Elizabethan architect Robert Smythson, added the present Great Hall as well as the structure to the south. By the end of the 1570s further developments had been completed on the east side. This included an enclosed courtyard to the east of the house and a gatehouse to give extra protection from the public road.

After the turn of the seventeenth century the west side of the mansion had also been developed, along with a gallery. With continuous enhancements, the next major change was the addition of several substantial bay windows to the south and symmetrical developments to the north side. Workshops and other outbuildings were developed to the south, again with an enclosed courtyard.

The renowned Capability Brown undertook some work at the estate in the 1770s. It was about this time that William Constable modernised the house. A new entrance adorned the east elevation with the family's coat of arms above. The height of the main walls were increased and the top floor windows were brought into the main structure of the house. By now the house was looking very much as it is seen today, but behind the external facade the ongoing battle to keep the property in good order has never stopped.

With the monumental changes that the twentieth century brought, the present owner, Sir John Chichester Constable negotiated a formula which transferred the ownership of Burton Constable Hall to a foundation trust set up with the help and support of English Heritage.

The new foundation working with other bodies have now taken over the renovation and upkeep of this vast house and collections of treasures within.

The parkland that surrounds the house was also developed over many years, with a large lake to the south west of the property. Various members of the family enriched the property with magnificent furniture and paintings, along with artefacts from their travels around the world.

The house and gardens are open to the public from spring to late summer and a thriving caravan site occupies an area to the west of the lake. Following the death of his wife Gay in 1989, Sir John still resides in the south wing of the property and naturally takes a keen interest in the ongoing work to the Hall and its treasures within.

Rise Hall, 5km to the north of Burton Constable is also a very impressive property located in the densely wooded Rise Park. Unlike Burton Constable, it is not owned by the original family, nor is it open to the public. Several lodges surround the estate which has been sold on a number of occasions in recent years.

Back on the rail trail and, like Skirlaugh, the station site at New Ellerby has a small car park. It is also surrounded by many pleasant country lanes and footpaths and can be used as a central base for the numerous circular walks and cycle rides in the vicinity.

Just after the station the line headed through a short cutting, however with the establishment of trees and undergrowth in this rather wet environment, the trail has been forced to follow a route along the top to the east of the old alignment. Like many of the stations along this line, the platforms were staggered each side of the road crossing. This configuration was adopted when the tracks were doubled forty years after the line was built and alleviated the need to relocate the goods sidings which were set out opposite the original platform and station buildings.

The next station is Whitedale station site which also has a small car park. Built 2km west of Withernwick village and 2km east of Rise Park, you again have the option of using this location for a number of short circular rambles as shown on the map.

Another 2km along the trail is the site of Sigglesthorne station. A public house is only a short distance form the trail at this point. This station was originally named Great Hatfield after the village just to the east of the railway. However another name change took place in LNER days due, this time, to a station sharing the same identity in

South Yorkshire. Curiously the village of Sigglesthorne is actually over 4km to the north west of the station site.

Like so many of the settlements along this railway route the village of Great Hatfield has a long and interesting history. It was once a much larger village and is home to a fine medieval cross which is well worth a short walk to view.

In just under 2km further along the trail is another station site. This was called Wassand and yet again this was not the station's original name! The nearby small hamlet it served is called Goxhill, however, Goxhill is also the name for a larger and better known village on the south bank of the Humber, so a name change again ensued early in the life of this rural line.

It should be remembered that before the 1920s, almost every item of goods requiring transportation over land was most usually carried by the railways so, in the days before such new-fangled things as postcodes, the duplication of station names created very real problems. This became more apparent after the grouping of the railway companies into the 'Big Four' in 1922. If the new company had several stations bearing the same name it could find itself with major inefficiencies on its hands. By chance the Hornsea branch seemed to have been particularly unlucky in that it had a number of settlements on the Holderness Plain with similar names to other villages in the north of England.

Wassand station took its name from Wassand Hall which was over 2km from the station at the west side of Hornsea Mere. This station was only used on market days and faced closure in 1904. More footpaths abound in this area and offer easy circular walks whilst many quiet tarmac lanes make for splendid cycle routes devoid of the mud which can make off-road cycling unpleasant.

Now the trail has only another 3km to go before we reach the seafront at Hornsea. A kilometre on from Wassand and a long shallow cutting is entered where a road bridge crosses over the route at Southorpe. This was the site of another of the lost villages of the East Riding of Yorkshire. Believed to be of Danish origin, the settlement was to the west of the line and to the south of Hornsea Mere which can now been seen in all its splendour to the north of the trail.

Hornsea Mere has the surprising distinction of being the largest natural (as opposed to man made reservoirs) fresh water lake in Yorkshire. Formed from meltwater after the ice age, it is only a few metres deep but covers an area of several square kilometres to the west of the town of Hornsea. It is an outstanding area for bird life and a very important breeding site. Several footpaths enable you to wander around the lake, whilst the more energetic can take a boat out and row around this tranquil place which is less than a kilometre inland from the North Sea.

With developments along the railway the next station was by the B1242 road and called Hornsea Bridge station. Just before you reach this site the trail detours to the right as the old railway land has been used for housing. The original bridge and some of the embankment to the west side have also gone to provide space for this small development. Hornsea Bridge accommodated the main goods sidings for the town, leaving the passenger terminus free to handle the summer holiday traffic. The terminus was called Hornsea Town and was only a few metres from the sea.

You can still cover the last section from Hornsea Bridge to Hornsea Town station by climbing back up onto the embankment just beyond the new roundabout. The path covers around a kilometre where again a small housing development has taken shape. The original and majestic station buildings still remain, although now in private ownership, and the site of the old level crossing to give access to the carriage sidings can still be traced. The present path is to the east side of the station and brings you out with the seafront on your right. The last section is not suitable for cycles so the use of one of the roads running parallel to the old line is advised.

A benefit to passengers of bygone days was the proximity to the seafront of both Hornsea and Withernsea stations. A long struggle through busy town streets with numerous bags of luggage and excited children was not necessary. The sea was there, straight in front just as you climbed off the train. Unlike Withernsea, which only developed after the arrival of the railway, Hornsea was already an established settlement before the railway came in 1864. Naturally, some further enlargement took place, but it was never intended to transform the town into a mini Blackpool. The main street is a kilometre from the sea and has a number of attractive properties along with shops and places to obtain refreshments. A small museum covers many aspects of local life and can keep your interest on a wet day. To the south of the town is the well known Hornsea Pottery. Apart from the factory, this site has been developed as both a leisure and retail complex trading as Hornsea Freeport. It can be very busy and noisy at almost any time of the year but it has helped tremendously to bring visitors back to the town after the closure of the railway.

Generally the Hornsea Rail Trail is well maintained and is pleasingly free of abandoned rubbish. A few locations can become a little boggy in late winter and barriers to prevent the misuse of the trail by motor cycles have been erected in the Hull area. Overall this is an excellent route and for the average rambler wearing shorts on a summer's day, the worst problem to be encountered will be a few nettle stings! Most can put up with that in exchange for a pleasant days trek in the sunshine!

The Hornsea trail draws to a close the selection of railway walks from East Yorkshire. There are now just two main railway routes still open to all traffic in the county.

The first is the original railway line of 1840 which ran into the county from Selby. The second is the Hull to Scarborough line which was opened throughout in 1848. Both are still busy routes with regular services, although the Scarborough line is more of a commuter link since the decline of summertime excursion traffic. Also still open is the more direct link for London bound trains from Gilberdyke Junction on the Hull - Selby line. This route crosses the River Ouse by a multi-span swing bridge to the east of Goole, then proceeds south west to Doncaster where it joins the East Coast Main Line. As mentioned, sections of the former Hull and Barnsley high level route that encircles the city of Hull still sees regular freight traffic to and from the eastern docks and the BP Chemicals plant at Saltend a little further east.

After many years of decline the third Millennium shows signs of a railway renaissance in the UK, and East Yorkshire is no exception. A new private railway operator in the area is setting out its stall to provide a number of daily direct services to London Kings Cross and freight traffic to the eastern docks is now at its busiest for decades. The East Coast Main Line is also reaping the benefits of full electrification and is, in turn encouraging significant discussion about similar investment to modernise the trans-Pennine route to Liverpool. Locally too, there are proposals to build a railway halt 1km west of Paragon Station in Hull to serve a new sports stadium scheme at Anlaby Road Cricket Circle and other ideas include new modern commuter stops near to Melton and Beverley. As our roads become increasingly congested, failing to deliver the necessary required capacity because of economic cutbacks and environmental fears, are we to see a real return to the railways as a sensible alternative means of transport?

We are unlikely to see a return to the country railway again, but maybe the future of the lines we do still have looks far more secure than it has done for many years.

Maybe, just maybe, the tide is turning?

Fact File: The Hornsea Rail Trail.

Start/Finish: Central or North East Hull to Hornsea.
Grid Refs: TA 106302 to TA 208477. A well used trek from city to coast with only one major road crossing, (A165 near Skirlaugh).
Location: Industrial Hull off Mount Pleasant (A1033) to Hornsea seafront.
Max. length of walk: 21km (13 miles), typical walking time 5 hours plus, one way.
Length of shorter walk: 13km (8 miles), typical time 3 hours, from A165 near Skirlaugh to Great Hatfield and back.
OS maps: Landranger 106, Pathfinder 687, 676 & 677, (TA 03/13, TA 04/14 & TA 23/24).
Points of interest: Burton Constable Hall, Hornsea Mere, Hornsea Pottery. All the normal seaside facilities available at the coast. Several shops and good pubs quite close to the trail.
Tourist information office: Hornsea, (seasonal office open in summer months only), Tel: (01964) 536404, also Hull City Centre. Tel: (01482) 223559.
Cycling: This is a generally well maintained route. You can cover the full length with no more than a few nettle stings in mid summer. Many quiet lanes between New Ellerby and Hornsea Mere make for pleasant circular options.

Chapter 7

Along Yorkshire's Clifftops.

Walk 10. Rail Trail to Whitby.

We now move north and sample two dramatic former railway lines that clung to the rugged coast line of the northern part of the County of Yorkshire.

The Scarborough and Whitby Railway and the Whitby, Redcar and Middlesbrough Union Railway formed a coastal link that once provided a direct rail link from Hull on the River Humber to Middlesbrough on the River Tees. Whilst the route was continuous, no through train service was ever scheduled over the full length but passengers could have made the full trip at one time with just a change of train at Scarborough.

The first trail considered is the 30km long route north from Scarborough to Ravenscar, Robin Hoods Bay and over the Esk Valley to Whitby West Cliff. The early efforts to connect the coastal towns of Scarborough with Whitby and Whitby with Loftus and Saltburn (already linked by railway to Redcar and Middlesbrough), appear not to have been based on sound economics. Approaches by the local communities had been made to the North Eastern Railway Company to construct these lines, but they fell on very deaf ears.

Certainly the mighty railway companies did not see their role as filling social needs to link small struggling communities to the main railway system. Nor were government subsidies available in Victorian Britain to help build new transport links.

In this particular area the NER viewed such a line as having low traffic potential which could possibly even take business away from their existing routes to Whitby and Scarborough. Additionally, like so many coastal railways, the projected route posed many engineering difficulties which would not be easy to overcome unless substantial amounts of money were spent.

In consequence it was left to local groups to raise the necessary capital and drum up support to achieve the link. After several failed attempts in the 1860s, it was in the 1870s that some action finally occurred. The owner of the isolated Raven Hall, a Mr W. H. Hammond, was a prominent driving force behind making this stretch of the Yorkshire coast more accessible and he is associated as one of the leading protagonists of the line. At about this time there were proposals to develop the areas around Ravenscar (known as Peak, until the turn of last century) and Robin Hoods Bay into fashionable holiday spa towns. Attempts to develop land around the village of Ravenscar are well documented, but in the event only the Station Square received buildings on one side before depression hit the area and put an end to the many grand plans of that era.

The plan for the railway was for a completely independent line commencing with a station to the north side of Scarborough in an area known as Gallows Close. The route then headed north to a terminus on the south side of the River Esk at Whitby and thus having no connections to any of the existing railway lines.

Work began in 1872 but with little over 10km of the railway constructed by 1873, funds finally dried up and the work stopped. It was to be another twelve years before the complete route was finally opened, though this was to a new alignment which connected with other railways at both ends. A short tunnel at Falsgrave, at the southern end of the line, took the tracks through to a junction with the main NER tracks just west of Scarborough station. At the northern end, a fine red brick viaduct carried the single track railway high over the River Esk at Larpool to make an end on junction with the recently opened route up to Loftus and Saltburn.

The operation of this railway, officially opened on 16th July 1885, proved to be notoriously difficult throughout its history. Like the railway to Loftus, the route had a succession of very steep gradients. The climb up to Ravenscar from the south was 1 in 41 and 1 in 39 from the north. In railway terms these were amongst some of the steepest gradients to be found anywhere on a standard gauge railway line in this country.

The weather contributed to operational problems too. With the rugged coastline close by, frequent sea frets would descend and create adhesion difficulties on the wet rails. Add that to the damp tunnels located on the most difficult parts of the route and you had a formula which stretched the skill and ability of many a locomotiveman as he battled hard to keep his train on time.

Man made operational problems existed at either end of the route where reversal of the complete train was necessary to gain entry to the main stations at Scarborough and Whitby Town. Certainly a most inefficient manoeuvre in the days of steam locomotive power.

Yorkshire Railway Rambles 1. North and East

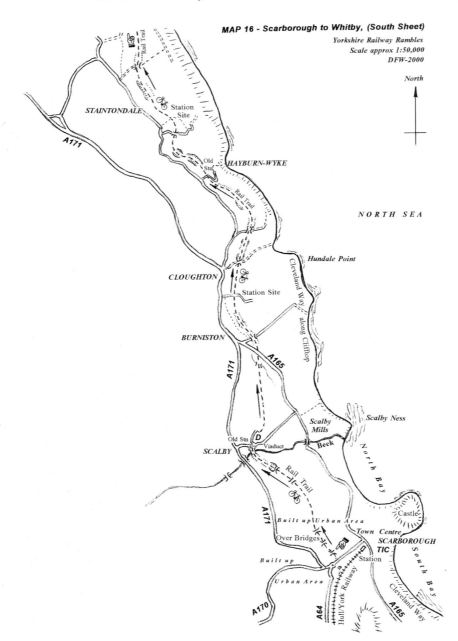

MAP 16 - Scarborough to Whitby, (South Sheet)

Yorkshire Railway Rambles
Scale approx 1:50,000
DFW-2000

North

STAINTONDALE

Station
Site

A171

Old
Stn

HAYBURN-WYKE

Rail Trail

NORTH SEA

Hundale Point

CLOUGHTON

Cleveland Way along Clifftop

Station Site

BURNISTON

A171

A165

Scalby
Mills

Scalby Ness

Old Stn

D

SCALBY

Viaduct

Beck

North Bay

Rail Trail

A171

Built up Urban Area

Castle

Over Bridges

Town Centre

SCARBOROUGH

TIC

Built up

Station

South Bay

Urban Area

A170

A64

Hull/York Railway

A165

Cleveland Way

Along Yorkshire's Clifftops

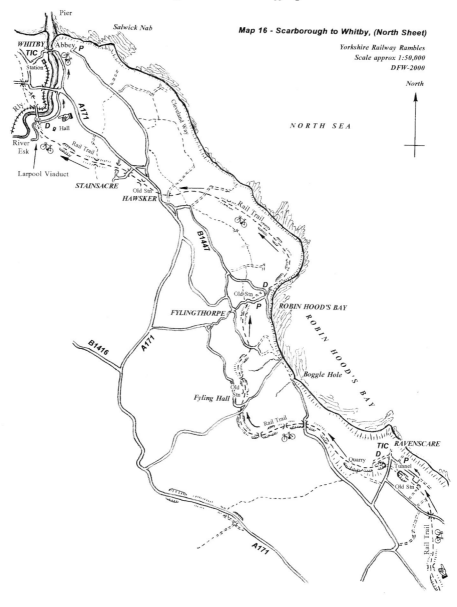

Map 16 - Scarborough to Whitby, (North Sheet)

Yorkshire Railway Rambles
Scale approx 1:50,000
DFW-2000

North

Pier

Salwick Nab

WHITBY
TIC

Abbey P

Station

Rly

D Hall

River
Esk

Rail Trail

Larpool Viaduct

STAINSACRE

Old Stn
HAWSKER

Cleveland Way

Rail Trail

B1447

NORTH SEA

Old Stn

D

P

FYLINGTHORPE

ROBIN HOOD'S BAY

B1416

A171

Boggle Hole

ROBIN HOOD'S BAY

Old
Stn

Fyling Hall

Rail Trail

Quarry

TIC RAVENSCARE
D
P

Tunnel

Old Stn

A171

Rail Trail

Yorkshire Railway Rambles 1. North and East

As with all railways to holiday destinations, the summer months would see almost every seat taken on each train by excited holiday makers, but for much of the rest of the year, just a few carriages would suffice to carry a handful of passengers.

With the start of the British Railways era, shortly after the Second World War, it became a difficult battle to retain these unprofitable lines along the coast. With many problematic viaducts and difficult tunnels, the line north from Whitby West Cliff station (which is covered in walk No. 11) closed in 1958. The Scarborough to Whitby route continued for seven more years only to fall victim to the Beeching Plan of 1963. The route closed on 6th March 1965 and the track was lifted soon afterwards.

Although hardly ever profitable, it is such a tragedy that the line did not survive. It was renowned for its stunning coastal views, especially the stretch around the magnificent sweep of Robin Hoods Bay. Yet the idea of developing it into a long distant path followed a very slow programme, in fact taking longer than it took to plan and build the line a century earlier! Indeed, over thirty years would pass before it was possible to walk and cycle the majority of this fine scenic route.

The original line commenced about 1km to the south west of Scarborough station with a junction heading north through Falsgrave tunnel. Like the tunnel at Ravenscar, this short structure, 238 metres in length, was built by the 'cut and cover' method. This is where a cutting is first excavated for the railway, then after forming the brick archway, covered over again to either hide the line from view, or, as in built up areas, to alleviate the obstacle of a railway in a town. The area north of the tunnel at Gallows Close was developed by the NER as a goods shed and sidings in 1900-1902.

This area, north of Falsgrave Road (the A64 trunk road), has now been swallowed up by a large modern supermarket development. The extensive site has the usual huge car park and petrol station with the access off Falsgrave Road itself, close to the start of Westborough which continues towards Scarborough town centre and the still impressive railway station facade.

The northbound walk begins here amidst the bustle of central Scarborough. As you head north on foot or on cycle and through the supermarket car park you will see the first of many bridges which you will pass beneath en route. The bridge spans are quite wide on this section of the trek as they once crossed over three or four parallel railway tracks. Although much graffiti is in evidence in this urban section, the trek is quite clear and well maintained, as is the situation throughout most of the route.

After passing beneath three bridges a large cemetery is passed on your right (east). If you are on a cycle you will need to go along the road here and turn right, getting back on to the trek after a few hundred metres. Urban developments slowly start to give way to greener fields over the next 2km or so. Although built to double track width at this point the two tracks were actually operated as two independent single lines, with one line extending only as far as Northstead carriage sidings laid out in 1908.

Shortly after this site and the red brick viaduct over Scalby Beck appears as we leave the northern environs of Scarborough town.

Just to the north of the viaduct a short deviation from the line of the railway has been signed, bringing you out onto Station Road, left into Field Close Road, then right along Lancaster Way. At the end of this residential road the course of the former railway is re-joined and after a slight left hand bend, a long straight section takes you due north to Burniston. The A165 needs to be crossed with care, then it is back into the greenery of the trek winding gently northwards.

The trek now follows several kilometres of shallow cuttings and low embankments with plenty of bushes, wild flowers and young trees along the route. Frequent country lanes provide plenty of opportunities to pause and enjoy some light refreshments along the way. Some are well established watering holes, while other entrepreneurial types, having spotted the popularity of this trek on hot summer days, have appeared at various points along the trail to provide teas, snacks and ice creams for weary walkers and cyclists!

With the former station site north of the viaduct at Scalby completely vanished under new residential development, it is pleasing to see that almost every part of Cloughton station buildings remain.

Tables and chairs cover the area where trains once stopped between the platforms and a thriving refreshment trade is conducted throughout the summer months. Pass to the west side of the main station buildings, then back onto the trek by the site of the former level crossing.

It is a further 2km north along the woodland shrouded track to the site of Hayburn Wyke station. Although the single platform remains beneath the undergrowth, the wooden station buildings have been swept away. Another opportunity exists here for a pint at the nearby hotel, just to the south of the line. Here also an enjoyable diversion down to the sea at Hayburn Wyke bay can be taken where the main path of the Cleveland way is joined. The next 2km takes you further along to the site of the of Staintondale station. Here the buildings and platforms at the west side of the trek remain intact but are now a private residence.

It is not very often that you are aware of a slope when you are cycling or walking along an old railway track, but the ascent to the summit of this line at Ravenscar is an exception.

With a 1 in 41 gradient approach from the south you can clearly see the rise of the track bed in front of you. This was one of the most notorious gradients on the North Eastern Railway with locomotives struggling hard on the wet rails. This often necessitated the use of a banking engine to provide assistance at the rear of the train, or an extra engine at the front to double head the trains. Both were a frequent sight in the summer months.

The site of Ravenscar station is reached after a further 2km. The grand plan to develop Peak, as Ravenscar was originally called, into a smart Victorian holiday town went only as far as the construction of the buildings to the north side of the Station Square. You must turn to the east of the original station to face the three story buildings where again refreshments can be obtained. The track onward through the station and down through the short tunnel are fenced off for safety reasons. Take the wide Station Road northwards to the imposing entrance of the Raven Hall Hotel. Here the road turns sharp left, while the trek takes the path at 45 degrees to the left and passes the National Trust Shop and Information Point. The National Trust own various parts of the rugged sea cliffs and old quarry sites along the North Yorkshire Coast. This is a very active charity and is custodian of much more than just a few old houses in the south east! Special effort is made to preserve all aspects of the wildlife and plants along these stretches of coastline, so do spend a few minutes, and pounds inside their shop!

Ravenscar is well worth a short stop over and if time permits a trip down to the beach along well worn paths can be rewarding. This section of the coast is renown for fossils and almost every piece of rock can be broken open to reveal an ancient ammonite shell.

Back on the main path and after a short bumpy decent the line of the railway is rejoined just past the northern portal of the old tunnel.

A Southbound Train Climbing Ravenscar Bank

At 255 metres in length the tunnel was constructed on a tight curve as the line climbed up to the summit by the station. You now have the benefit of a falling gradient and the spectacular view out across Robin Hoods Bay. Large disused quarry sites are to your left whilst the ground falls away steeply to the sea cliffs to your right. Drink in the marvellous view as you meander north westwards towards Fyling Hall station site.

With the removal of the old bridge over the road, you enter the former station site through a heavily wooded section of the line. The buildings are a private residence at the west side of the track. The next few kilometres of the trail have kept the local council busy in maintaining a safe passage as parts of the old embankments have collapsed. Great care is required here and children should be kept well away from any land slips. At the time of writing, tenders are been sought to rectify this problem, but please take heed of any safety warning notices that may advise you to follow a short diversion.

You now steadily approach the north side of this scenic bay and enter the site of what was the most important intermediate station on the line, that of Robin Hoods Bay. The large station site is predominantly a car park now with toilet facilities and many nearby shops. The bridges over the roads to each side of the station have been removed, so a short turn right, then left, brings you past the old station buildings and into the car park.

The village is one of the Yorkshire coast's marvellous little gems and a walk down into the old part amidst the cobble streets and then out onto the rocky shoreline is a joy in itself. Although a very popular, and sometimes very busy haunt for day trippers there are still pleasant restaurants and traditional pubs to be found for a spot of well earned relaxation.

Back onto the trail however and at the north end a detour along the residential road opposite the station site is required, and again, a sort of zig-zag, left then right, is necessary to get back onto the old trackbed.

Hereon and a number of short cuttings take the trail 5km around the exposed headland, much of which is owned by the National Trust, and then back inland again and onto High Hawsker. The road bridge that carried the A171 over the rails has been demolished and care crossing this busy road is required just before the old station site is reached. Again refreshments are available here where once only tickets to travel on the trains were the order of the day. After walking alongside

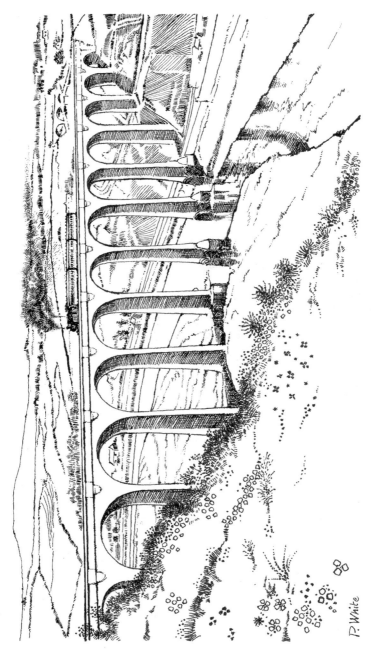

Crossing Larpool Viaduct, Whitby c.1930s

P. White

the busy road for a kilometre, the tracks pass under a small bridge and slowly leave the main road on your right.

Trees and hedges cover much of the line side again as it is less exposed to the gales that blow off the North Sea. A further 3km takes you up to the impressive Larpool Viaduct which spans the Esk Valley and where, to your right, Larpool Hall comes into view. This is a large stone built country mansion house that was once dominant in this area.

The red brick viaduct stands as yet another massive monument to our Victorian railway builders. At 279 metres in length, it stands over 38 metres high and the thirteen graceful arches are said to contain over five million bricks! Now, alas, the structure stands idle and a high metal fence bars the passage of even a solitary walker, let alone a hundred tonnes of mighty locomotive!

The structure not only crosses the tidal River Esk, but also the tracks of the original Whitby to Pickering Railway on the north bank which is still in use as a single track branch to Battersby Junction and Middlesborough. It also crosses the trackbed of the steeply graded spur line from Whitby Town station up to Prospect Hill junction where the Scarborough line once joined the existing tracks to Whitby West Cliff station. It was here that trains from Scarborough had once more to reverse direction in order to gain access to Whitby Town station.

But for now we cannot cross the viaduct and to complete the trek into Whitby the track bed has to be left behind. Just prior to the start of the viaduct there is a narrow lane which takes the route eastward for 2km and into the centre of town.

Whitby has a bustling centre with an array of shops, restaurants and pubs. Moreover the town has an interesting history and a number of cultural sites worth visiting including the ruin of the 11th century Benedictine abbey destroyed following the dissolution of the monasteries by Henry VIII. The first abbey built on this bracing cliff top site high above the town founded in 657 by the Saxon Princess, St. Hilda. It was destroyed by the Vikings around 866 and rebuilt by the Normans in 1078.

The old harbour area with the long twin jetties sheltering the entrance to the River Esk are also worthy of a stroll.

All in all this route is a very pleasant days walk or cycle ride. Equally it can be combined with a couple of overnight stops, allowing leisurely visits to many of the interesting places en route. If however

Whitby Abbey

you have taken the day to make the journey then a bus trip back to Scarborough and the starting point is now required, it's just a pity that there is no train to take you back!

Fact File: Rail Trail to Whitby

Start/Finish: Scarborough to Whitby
Grid Refs: TA 035882 & NZ 897095 (or NZ 900111 - town centre). An excellent railway trek with spectacular sea views.
Location: North side of A64 Falsgrave Road (new supermarket site) to Larpool Viaduct south side of the River Esk (2km takes you into Whitby town centre).
Max. length of walk: 35km (22 miles), typical walking time, one way, 7 hours plus.
Length of shorter walk: 15km (9 miles), Ravenscar to Robin Hoods Bay and return, typical time 3 to 4 hours,
OS maps: Landranger 94 & 101, Outdoor Leisure 27, (North York Moors Eastern sheet).
Points of interest: Castle, Abbey, Cliffs and Harbours, this walk has an array of points to interest all the family, (even amusement arcades!). Several toilets en route along with cafes, pubs and shops. Several old stations serve refreshments.
Tourist information office: Scarborough, Tel: (01723) 373333 and Whitby, Tel: (01947) 602674.
Cycling: Generally this scenic route is well maintained and safe for bikes. Please follow council instructions at times of repair, as land slips can be an ongoing problem on any route so close to cliff tops. Also please show consideration for walkers as several sections can become very busy during the summer months.

Walk 11. The Sandsend Ness Spectacular.

The railway that linked Loftus to Whitby was a quite remarkable structure. With the grand title of 'The Whitby, Redcar and Middlesbrough Union Railway', it opened just before its southern neighbour in 1883. To railwaymen it was one of the most difficult stretches to operate. Like the Scarborough to Whitby line, it too had many severe gradients and a succession of viaducts over many deep river valleys. It also had three difficult tunnels, one of which had a reputation that even the most experienced locomotivemen would dread on a wet misty morning.

Sandsend tunnel was just over a kilometre in length. A single track tunnel, it had a severe gradient throughout. It was linked by just a short length of exposed track, on a shelf high above the North Sea, to the shorter Kettleness tunnel. This few kilometres of track were not for the faint hearted. With little opportunity to gather any speed after leaving Sandsend station, a heavy steam train would struggle into the tunnel belching smoke and steam. Once inside the air would become acrid with the engine exhaust as the wheels slipped away on the greasy wet rails. Enginemen have told of trains literally sliding backwards on the gradient as they failed to pull the heavy train through.

Inside the confined space the smoke, steam, and soot could bring the train crew to their knees, gasping for fresh air in the black confine. Even with more powerful modern locomotives the Sandsend tunnel never lost its awesome reputation throughout the operational history of the line. Little doubt that these operational difficulties, plus the expensive upkeep of the many viaducts, did not help the case for keeping this line open. It closed in 1958 even before the Beeching report had scrutinised all the branch lines in North Yorkshire.

Like the Scarborough to Whitby railway it too was promoted by an independent company. They had high hopes that the mineral wealth along the line of the railway would generate considerable freight traffic. Although many mines and quarries did open as a result of this line, they never produced the level of traffic needed to justify this expensive railway.

The original company ran out of funds before the completion of the route leaving the North Eastern Railway Company to finish the job. Their engineers considered the line to be so poorly constructed that many sections had to be dismantled and re-built. Indeed one section of the line had been planned to run on a narrow shelf high above the North Sea but part of this earthworks collapsed into the sea during construction and the NER realigned the route through the Sandsend and Kettleness tunnels.

The many high viaducts on the line had been designed by Thomas Booch. He was responsible for the original ill fated Tay Bridge which collapsed in a violent storm on the last day of 1879. Consequently many of the viaducts on this route were re-built, or re-designed with

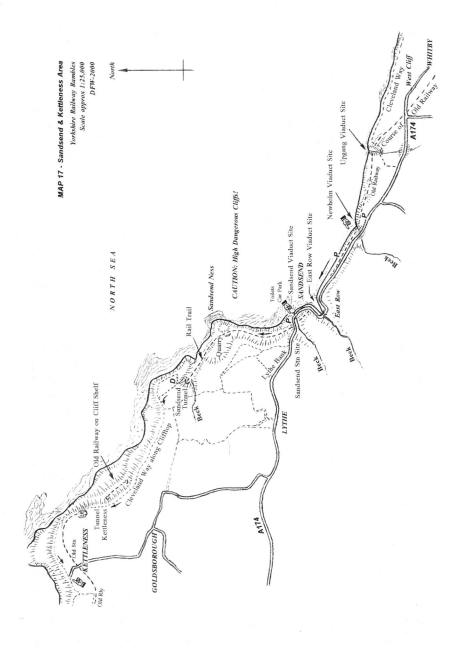

MAP 17 - Sandsend & Kettleness Area
Yorkshire Railway Rambles
Scale approx 1:25,000
DFW-2000

North

NORTH SEA

WHITBY

Cleveland Way

West Cliff

Old Railway

A174

Course of

Old Railway

Upgang Viaduct Site

Newholm Viaduct Site

P

P

Beck

Sandsend Viaduct Site

East Row Viaduct Site

SANDSEND

Sandsend Ness

CAUTION: High Dangerous Cliffs!

Toilets

Car Park

P

East Row

Beck

Beck

Rail Trail

Quarry

Sandsend Stn Site

Lythe Bank

Beck

Old Railway on Cliff Shelf

D

Sandsend

Tunnel

Beck

LYTHE

A174

Cleveland Way along Clifftop

Tunnel

Kettleness

Old Stn

KETTLENESS

Old Rly

GOLDSBOROUGH

extra bracing to ensure adequate strength against the fierce north winds off the sea. So it was many years after the planned opening that the first trains finally ran.

This walk takes in the short but very scenic stroll from the site of Newholm Beck viaduct to the tunnel entrance north of Sandsend Ness. You can park alongside the A174 road from Whitby to Saltburn and Middlesbrough. The road has been widened at the site of the viaduct to East Row taking up part of the railway land where it ran between the road and the sea. It is just under a kilometre from Newholm Beck to East Row Beck, where another viaduct carried the single track railway over the road and stream, then behind the row of houses at the other side of the beck.

You have to walk inland and over the narrow road bridge, before returning to the sea front. In a short distance you come to another stream which again required a substantial viaduct for the railway to cross over to the site of Sandsend station. A further large car park is located between the station and the sea giving you the option of starting the walk from here.

Steps lead up from the car park to the level of the railway above. The station buildings remain as a private residence. Turn to your right and start to follow the track of the railway. To your right is the sea below, while to your left the cliffs are actually the remains of a succession of quarries excavated into the hill side. Many old spoil heaps exist which also add to the landscape. In view of its location and so much quarry activity over the years, this section of the trackbed can be somewhat unstable. Do take care here as small land slips still regularly occur.

The route continues to gain height and Sandsend Ness is passed before the track bed curves to the left. Marked walkways enable the exploration of some of the old quarry workings, but care must be taken for obvious reasons. Walking north west and the wooded cliffs dominate the view in front. The sea then slips out of sight as a short cutting is entered just prior to the Sandsend tunnel entrance.

The tunnel is not a safe place to enter, but stand by the portal and feel the icy rush of air on even the hottest day. The walk need not end here as the Cleveland Way long distance footpath now climbs up the very steep steps to the right. This leads to the top of the cliffs and a path further along the coast. Glimpses of the spectacular trackbed shelf between the tunnels, where the railway once perched half way down the cliffs, are obtainable just over a kilometre further to the north west.

The path effectively bypasses the tunnels such that the northern portal of Kettleness tunnel is now about 2km from the southern portal of Sandsend tunnel. The site of Kettleness is soon reached which once served the small hamlet here. However in the early part of the nineteenth century Kettleness was a thriving fishing village not unlike Staithes until tragedy struck the community. A massive land slip sent much of the village crashing into the North Sea below.

For walkers tackling the long distance Cleveland Way footpath, you are never far from much of the route of the old railway. After Kettleness is Runswick Bay, then Hinderwell and then on to Staithes. Here just north of the station is this site where the massive Staithes viaduct was built. The original stone abutments can still be seen across the valley. It was a typical Thomas Bouch design of slender cast iron columns. However extra cross bracing was ordered by the Board of Trade Inspector before it was opened to traffic. At over 300 metres in length and over 30 metres at its highest point, the structure had to withstand the full force of any North Sea storms and was equipped with a special wind gauge. If the gauge's alarm bell sounded in the nearby signal box, all traffic had to be suspended over the viaduct until the wind subsided. With the Tay Bridge disaster too fresh in the country's mind, bridge safety was a priority in the early 1880s. In fact the collapse of Bouch's Tay bridge structure brought ruination upon him. He had been knighted just months earlier by Queen Victoria but died in the following year.

A little further north of this very deep valley is the modern day potash mine at Boulby. The railway re-appears here as a mineral line serving the mine where a huge silo has been erected to load bogie wagons with the excavated mineral. The track itself first runs inland and through Grinkle tunnel, then on past Loftus, on the original railway alignment, and over Kilton embankment. Years ago this was once an impressive viaduct with eleven masonry piers but mining subsidence in 1911 meant that it had to be hurriedly converted into a solid structure. It was thus buried under thousands of tonnes of spoil to make it into a safe embankment.

Just beyond this former massive structure was a junction which gave access to an unusual 'zig zag' of tracks taking the lines down the steep hillside to reach sea level at Skinningrove. The current freight

Train on Newholm Beck Viaduct c.1950s

only line continues over the A174 on a new concrete and steel viaduct then past the Skinningrove steel works. This has also brought much traffic to the line over the years.

The line heads back towards the sea where is perched spectacularly on the clifftop at Huntcliff before heading inland again to Brotton and over the majestic Skelton brick viaduct hiding amongst the trees.

It is only a short distance now to the junction with the still used passenger line into Saltburn station. The Cleveland Way path enters the resort from the cliffs at the opposite side to the railway.

The whole route from Scarborough to Saltburn is never more than a few hundred metres from the cliff edge and makes for one of the most bracing railway walks in the country. Certainly if you have the time, spend four to five days covering the full length along the coast and all the little short walks too. However with the Sandsend Ness walk you can return to your transport from the tunnel portal near Sandsend by retracing your steps, or take in the 'way marks' through the old quarries. The view back across Sandsend Bay with Whitby beyond is wondrous on a clear day, and even in a storm, it is a spectacle to behold with waves crashing onto the cliffs far below.

Fact File: Sandsend Ness Spectacular

Start/Finish: Newholm Beck or Sandsend.

Grid Refs: NZ 871123 or NZ 861129. A bracing walk above the North Sea.

Location: A174 3km north west of Whitby.

Max. length of walk: 10km (7 miles) circular, typical walking time 3 hours.

Length of shorter walk: 6km (4 miles) circular, typical walking time 2 hours.

OS maps: Landranger 94, Outdoor Leisure 27, North York Moors Eastern sheet.

Points of interest: Old quarry workings, sites of viaducts and tunnels. Toilets, shops, cafes and pubs in Sandsend. As with all cliff top walks, please take special care if you have young children or animals with you, especially near to the old quarry workings.

Tourist information office: Whitby, Tel: (01947) 602674.

Cycling: This route is not suitable for cycles.

Kettleness Tunnel

Chapter 8

Moorland Rail Routes

Walk 12. Climbing to Goathland

The final selection of routes take us inland, away from the coast and onto the exalted upland wilderness known as the North Yorkshire Moors. Some 10km along the Esk valley, upstream from Whitby is the village of Grosmont. This settlement lies on the original route of the Whitby to Pickering Railway, one of the earliest railways built in this country and which opened in 1836. Originally, horses provided the power along this single track railway which ran along the Esk valley and then up and over the bleak moors before descending to the town of Pickering. Although the horse drawn railway was a massive boost to the local communications and economies almost two centuries ago, the emerging power of the steam locomotive was soon recognised as the way forward.

The independent line was purchased by George Hudson's rapidly growing York and North Midland Railway network in 1845. The new owners immediately set about re-building the line to take the weight of steam locomotives and to make it into double track. This resulted in the replacement of many of the bridges and re-alignment of some sections to reduce the number of sharp curves. It also resulted in a new tunnel at Grosmont opened in 1847.

The engineer for the original line was non other than George Stephenson and he had designed a small single bore tunnel just to the south of Grosmont station to take the line under the adjacent hill. This still remains today for use by pedestrians and runs alongside the present double track tunnel.

Steam locomotive hauled trains commenced services in 1847, but with one noticeable exception.

To overcome the problem of raising the track level from the Esk valley floor to the top of the Yorkshire moors on the original railway, Stephenson had constructed a rope hauled incline between the villages of Beck Hole and Goathland.

Rope inclines were common on early railways and the systems involved a fixed winding engine positioned at the summit of a steep incline (usually with a gradient of around 1 in 5). This then used a rope or cable to pull up around half a dozen wagons at a time. Often

Moorland Rail Routes

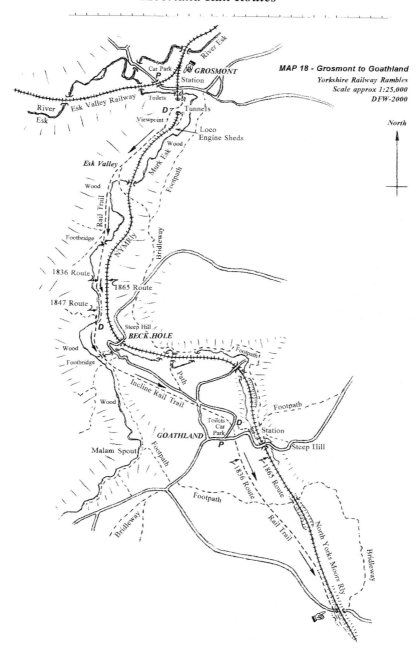

MAP 18 - Grosmont to Goathland
Yorkshire Railway Rambles
Scale approx 1:25,000
DFW-2000

North

wagons going in the opposite direction would be used as a counter weight and descend the incline as the other wagons were raised. Naturally a passing loop, or a twin track incline, was required.

In theory the systems worked adequately, but as railways became more advanced and had more demands placed upon them, rope worked inclines were seen as a hindrance to fast and efficient operation. They also provided the potential for serious accidents, such as in the event of a cable snapping or a coupling breaking. Sadly just such an accident occurred on this incline in 1864 when the last coach of a passenger train broke free and careered down the bank. Two passengers lost their lives and a further thirteen were injured. It became inevitable that an alternative to the rope hauled incline was required. The North Eastern Railway thus opened a new 8km long route from just east of the existing line at Grosmont to Ellerbeck south of Goathland. The gradient of the new line at 1 in 49 was still steep, but could be tackled satisfactorily by the ever improving design of steam locomotives.

The effect of the new route, which was opened in 1865, was to leave 8km of disused track which included the incline. Surprisingly, although services ceased that year, the North Eastern Railway did not have the tracks lifted. With local pressure to keep a service to Beck Hole village, at the foot of the old incline, some provision was retained for freight to be collected and ironstone from nearby drift mines.

Following local pressure, the NER started a limited passenger service from Grosmont to Beck Hole, hoping to capitalise on day trippers to the area. Started in 1908, the Great War saw the end of this train after only six years.

So almost a century has passed since this part of the line was finally abandoned. It is along this old trackbed that this walk follows most of the length of the original 1836 route, including the incline.

Naturally you can start at either end, but I have described the route from Grosmont southwards. With the facilities of the North Yorkshire Moors Railway making Grosmont a popular destination for visitors, a large car park and picnic area has been created to the west of the village. The main street through the village is not suitable for long term parking so use of the car park is essential. The main public railway along the Esk valley still operates a regular service stopping at Grosmont station with trains en route from Middlesbrough to Whitby town. The North Yorkshire Moors Railway, currently the country's largest preserved line, uses the main part of Grosmont station as their northern terminus. Throughout the summer it is alive with steam trains and is a vivid reminder of just how noisy it was to live close to a railway in the days of steam. Constant whistles signal the train crew's actions, accompanied by clanking of carriage and wagon buffers as trains are shunted about. The general hustle and bustle which was once an everyday scene at thousands of wayside stations across the length and breadth of the country is saved for posterity

Trains run throughout most of the year along this preserved railway. An army of enthusiasts and volunteers keep the line going and the company has a large workshop and museum to the south of the village accessed via a footpath through the original 1836 tunnel.

This walk takes the path to the left of the tunnels and passes the small church of St Matthews on the left. Turning first right and over the top of both the tunnels, you then take the gate to the left and down to the west side of the railway on the other side of the hill. A few viewing areas have been set out here to allow people to take photographs of the trains in action.

The route passes by the workshops and sidings where many old locomotives, carriages and wagons await restoration. The railway lines slowly curve to the left to climb the route of the 1865 deviation whilst the path continues almost flat along the course of the original

route. A row of cottages at the small hamlet of Esk Valley are on the left, whilst the site of an ironstone mine is on the right. The flowing waters of the Murk Esk are never far away from the old railway and like its bigger brother, the River Esk, has to be crossed several times.

The valley is quite wooded for most of the route to the incline. The river is crossed next on a timber footway which uses the old stone piers of the original railway bridge. On the next section, the deviation line is above and to the left whilst the Murk Esk is to the right. Continuing your walk you stay on the east bank of the stream, although here, the first re-alignment of 1847 crossed the Murk Esk twice in quick succession to straighten out the first horse drawn route of 1836. However, after years without maintenance the remains of the bridge here was washed away in 1930.

The thickly wooded area is called Buber Wood and was home to many mining families in the late 1850s. No trace of their cottages remain, only small spoil heaps from the drift mines and old furnaces are in evidence, though long since reclaimed by nature. The next bridge over the stream carried the tracks back onto the route of this walk and now caters for walkers taking another footpath west and into the woods. At this point there are two footpaths ahead of you. The left hand one takes you into the tiny community of Beck Hole, while the right hand one is the continuation of the rail trail. After a few hundred metres you pass the site of the station that served Beck Hole village in the early years of the twentieth century.

Both a new footbridge and stepping stones let you cross the next small beck to the bank foot where trains waited to ascend the incline. You can also make use of the two footpaths to the east which provide a short walk to the stone bridge in Beck Hole and an opportunity to visit the small inn at the roadside!

The start of the broad incline rises over the next kilometre to Goathland. Stephenson's original incline design of 1836 was gravity worked. A long hemp rope was attached to water tanks mounted on wagons at the top of the incline. This rope then went around a 3 metre diameter fixed wheel and down to the bottom of the incline where it would be attached to a number of wagons or coaches. The weight of the water tank wagons hauled up the train as they descended to the incline bottom. The water was then emptied out and the tanks returned to the top again ready for the next duty. This rather crude system remained until the commencement of steam trains, when a static steam engine was installed at the incline top complete with new wire rope. The steady walk up the slope takes you over a minor road and into Goathland village. A short section from the incline top to the main street has been developed for housing, so a deviation along the road and past the public toilets and car park is neccessary. At the 'T' junction turn left, then right and back onto the course of the old line. The North Yorkshire Moors Railway station, built by the NER in 1865, is further along the road and, like Grosmont, can be a hive of activity.

Our walk now takes us south through 2km of grazing land with the deviation line steadily coming closer on the left. The Eller Beck continually crosses the path of the rails whilst the heather moors rise above on all sides. The trek finally ends next to the original gate keeper's cottage erected by the side of the road. The surviving rail route is carried over the road here on a stone bridge, rejoins the original 1836 route and continues to climb to the summit of the railway.

The walk has many circular options by combining with other footpaths in the area. A very pleasant route takes you behind the Mallyan hotel at the west end of Goathland village and down to the waterfall at Mallyan spout. The route then returns along the banks of the river to emerge in Beck Hole village back at the foot of the incline.

Walkers can of course make use of the trains, walking one way and catching the train back. No doubt those who may do this will catch the train up the hill and return down the gradient by foot!

It is a wonderful area with a lot of living history, thanks in no small part to the efforts of the hundreds of supporters of the North Yorkshire Moors Railway. Goathland has also become famous in recent years as the village of 'Aidensfield' in the popular Heartbeat TV programme. However, despite its popularity, mention should also be made of the local residents who both live and work here and who value their privacy.

The railway itself continues south and is well worth a trip aboard, not only to see other parts of the beautiful moors, but also to recapture the experience of the golden age of steam railways.

Join a sothbound train at Goathland and follow the line as it makes good use of the natural contours winding its course southward. At Eller Beck Bridge, the railway is carried over Fen Bog on the floor of a deep valley winding south and west. 5km south is Newtondale Halt, not far from the Saltergate Inn at the point on the A169 road known as the Devil's Elbow. However, no actual road links the railway halt to the inn. A further 5km south and the railway reaches the next station of Levisham.

This picturesque site is located in a densely wooded valley several kilometres from the village of Levisham and at a very different altitude. Road access down to Levisham station is through the villages of Lockton and Levisham, but be sure to check your brakes first!

The line now continues on to the southern terminus of the Railway at Pickering a further 8km away. Pickering station, like Goathland and Grosmont, can be another hive of activity with cafe and souvenir shop. The market town also has several interesting sites for the visitor including a castle which is under the guardianship of English Heritage and is open to the public.

A return trip on the train can now take you back to your original starting point at Grosmont.

Fact File: Climbing to Goathland

Start/Finish: Grosmont to Goathland or Moorgates.

Grid Refs: NZ 053828 & NZ 833013 or SE 845994. From the Esk valley to the edge of the moors.

Location: Grosmont station 4km west of A169 at Sleights to Goathland village centre, or south to Moorgates on road to Eller Beck Bridge.

Max. length of walk: 8km (5 miles), typical walking time 2 hours, one way. Several options to make circular route back to Grosmont, with a total distance of around 18km, (12 miles).

Length of shorter walk: 5km (3 miles), typical time 1 hour, in one direction.

OS maps: Landranger 94, Outdoor Leisure 27, North York Moors Eastern sheet.

Points of interest: Grosmont and Goathland railway stations are a hive of activity, (with toilets, shops and local public houses near by), plenty of moorland scenery as you steadily gain height.

Tourist information office: Whitby, Tel: (01947) 602674.

Cycling: The trail described is for walkers only, but a quick look at the OS map will not leave you short of ideas for a circular bike ride in this area.

Walk 13 - The Rosedale Iron Ore Circular

After the rolling hills on the Yorkshire Wolds and the flat plains of Holderness, we sampled the wooded slopes of the Esk valley and trekked along 40km of rugged coastline. Now let us sample the wild heather moors in the heart of North Yorkshire.

The North Yorkshire Moors is an area of outstanding natural beauty and at an average of over 400 metres above sea level experiences extremes of weather not often witnessed elsewhere. In winter the moors can be swept by deep drifting snow and a biting east wind, by summer they can be parched dry for weeks on end or transformed into a deep boggy morass after prolonged rain fall. Yet most weekends of the year see thousands of motorists and trippers heading for the moors to sample the delights of the locality. Fortunately, with such a large geographical area covered by the moors, it is still possible, even on the busiest days to find many quiet areas.

Between Castleton in the north and Hutton-le-Hole in the south is Rosedale. This is very much regarded as the heart of the moors. The dale itself is over 10km long with the River Seven rising close to Ralph's Cross at the watershed before flowing south through the full length of the dale. The small village of Rosedale Abbey nestles by the river, sheltered on three sides by the high moors. It is 6km from Hutton-le-Hole and accessed in that direction by very steep hill.

To look at the area today, you would probably be amazed to discover that a standard gauge railway system once ran along the tops of the moorland ridges. A century ago the complete dale was alive with industry, with railways on all three sides and numerous tramways and inclines feeding the main lines.

Smoke would have belched from the huge brick chimneys which accompanied dozens of furnaces working around the clock. This beautiful dale was a hive of industry and home to hundreds of mining families who had flocked to the area in search of work.

The mineral responsible for most of this activity was iron ore. Rosedale held many valuable seams beneath its coat of heather. Some quite readily accessible by quarrying and shallow drift mines, others only extracted through conventional mine shafts deep into the ground.

The mineral wealth deposited in the dale had been known about for many centuries but the quantities were not fully appreciated and this, combined with the difficult access to the area meant, that only

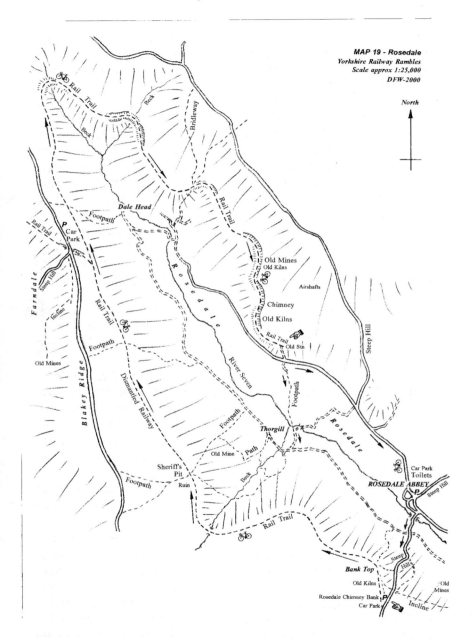

MAP 19 - Rosedale
Yorkshire Railway Rambles
Scale approx 1:25,000
DFW-2000

North

114

cottage scale extraction had previously taken place. However, as the industrial revolution took off in the first half of the nineteenth century, the expanding iron industry in and around Teeside developed an ever increasing appetite for raw materials. Rosedale, not surprisingly, came to the attentions of the industrialists and speculators.

In the 1850s large scale mining began a kilometre or so south of Rosedale Abbey and within five years the North Eastern Railway had opened its Rosedale Branch. Although the most logical route by rail out of the dale would have been south to the Vale of Pickering, the chosen route was north east, taking the railway over some of the highest and most exposed sections of the North Yorkshire Moors. This being the shortest route to transport the ore to its destination in the blast furnaces around the Tees.

The line commenced just south east of the village of Battersby, not far from the settlements of Great Ayton and Stokesley. The railway line branched south from the existing line passing close to the village of Ingleby where after only 3km, the notorious Ingleby Incline was ascended.

This was a rope hauled gradient 1.5 km long which raised the level of the railway from under 200 metres to over 400 metres above sea level. A large engine house was built at the bank top along with sidings and cottages for the railway workers.

Once atop the escarpment, the line actually took an almost level route, but twisting around the head of several dales in an eastwardly direction to reach Blakey Ridge. Here it passed under a stone road bridge where the tracks divided. One line ran around the west side of Rosedale to what became known as Chimney Bank Top, while the other line ran first north, around the head of the dale, and then swung back south to run along the east side of Rosedale.

With a total length of 32km, the complete system was fully open by August 1865 (the east branch opened four years later than the west branch).

This main railway was joined by a succession of further tramways and inclines from various new pits and mines as the industry developed. This also included a 2km incline down into Farndale. Cottages were built at many locations to house both the railway workers and their families and the quarry men and miners. The industry built a succession of furnaces at both sides of the dale along with other associated buildings and spoil heaps soon made their ugly appearance along with huge piles of calcine waste from the kilns. Curiously, years later it was realised that this waste product also had value and much of it was recovered and transported away for further processing.

In retropsect, particularly after so many decades, it is difficult to appreciate the level of industrial activity in this remote and enchanting location. That the industry was not destined to last was perhaps fortuitous, not only in that it returned the area back to nature, but that it provided an interesting and unusal heritage trail to follow.

The extraction of ore continued into the early years of the twentieth century but after several difficult years the general strike of 1926 saw the mining finish for the last time. Three further years passed during which time many tonnes of the calcine waste was removed and then, in 1929, the railway was officially closed and abandoned by the LNER.

With little alternative work in the area most families moved away and the extreme and severe weather of the moors assisted nature to landscape over many of the mining sites. Spoil heaps became covered with heather and the railway routes became grassed over. Redundant buildings were left to collapse or be plundered for their stone. Later still the newly formed National Park Authority further tided up some areas but also preserved for future generations some aspects of the industrial history. Much of the track bed of the former Rosedale Railway is now open for public access and it is along this route that we will take a closer look.

There are car parks at Blakey Ridge, Rosedale Chimney Bank Top and in Rosedale Abbey village. The latter can become very busy in summer months and it is best to avoid clogging up the village with cars. Bank Top is a better area to park up, as plenty of small parking areas exist. Blakey Ridge has the main Hutton-le-Hole to Castleton road passing along the top and a large car park exists where the railway once crossed under the road a kilometre south of the White Lion Inn.

The trackbed around Rosedale is open to walkers and cyclists, though parts of the East Branch are a little difficult to cycle along, due to subsidence and flooding in the cuttings. The stretch from Blakey to Ingleby is now footpath only and cycles are prohibited.

If we start our trek from Rosedale Chimney Bank Top, the logical direction is to cover the Rosedale section clockwise, although the trek does finish with a mighty hike up a 1 in 3 hill!

The old kilns mark the start of the route as we travel almost due north. A few cottages remain to your right and the village of Rosedale

Abbey 175 metres below in the valley. The track is excellent at the west side of the dale, level and well drained and you can make brisk progress 3km northward and westward until Sheriff's Pit is passed on your left. The opening to this 90 metre deep mine shaft is securely fenced off and a few stones remain of the Pithead manager's house close by. Lower down the dale side at Thorgill, drift mines linked into the operations at Sheriff's Pit.

Heading almost due north again it is just under 3km to Blakey Junction. Here the main line swung around to the west, under the road and on its journey to Ingleby Bank Top. We will take the other track, although still heading north for 2km and follow around the head of the dale. Gradually the route swings to the east, then to the south and along the top of the east flank of the dale. This section has seen the most damage from land slips and subsidence although is quite safe if treated with respect. Cyclists however may have difficulty staying in the saddle along several sections. Many of the cuttings are waterlogged so the path follows along the top edges.

After around 3km the first remains of the old kilns at the track side are passed. Various inclines are still visible which lead to drift mines and sidings. After the remains of more old kilns, which stand as monuments to the toils of the miners, an old chimney can be seen on the slopes above. On a clear day this is a beautiful trek. You can enjoy the splendid views across Rosedale without losing sight of the

harsh conditions and immense difficulties faced by a Victorian workforce as they earned a pitiful income. The dale has lost the grime and soot but the ghosts echo all around.

A bridleway crosses the old tracks close to Hill Cottages. Use this route down to Daleside Road, the narrow lane that leads a few kilometres up from the valley floor. Turning left (south east) it is a kilometre down to the junction with Knott Road and a further kilometre down to Rosedale Abbey village itself. Here a number of shops, an inn and public toilets are located around the small village green. You may need a few chocolate bars for energy as you now have to face a gruelling 1 in 3 climb back up to the top of Rosedale Chimney Bank.

Take the bridge over the River Seven sign posted for Hutton-le-Hole. After a short rise the second inn in the dale is passed on your left. Now take a deep breath and a long steady trudge up the steep bank. As your muscles ache with each step remember that several hundred men marched up this slope every day of the week in all weathers to work a full shift. Be thankful you can do it at your leisure and without a time clock at the top!

Fact File - Rosedale Iron Ore Circular.

Start/Finish: Rosedale Chimney Bank Top.
Grid Refs: SE 721947. A splended circular route around three flanks of Rosedale.
Location: Top of Rosedale Chimney Bank Top.
Max. length of walk: 18km (11 miles), typical time 4 hours.
Length of shorter walk: 11km (7 miles), typical walking time 3 hours, circular.
OS maps: Landranger 94, Outdoor Leisure 26 North York Moors Western sheet.
Points of interest: Old mines and kilns, wild moors. Shops, toilets and a good pub in Rosedale village.
Tourist information office: Hutton-le-Hole, (National Park Information Centre, seasonal opening), tel: (01751) 417367.
Cycling: The east side of this trek is in good order, but the west side is more difficult as some cuttings are flooded with the path around the top edge very steep in places. Please take care not to damage the fragile nature of this national park.

Walk 14 - Blakey Ridge to Incline Top and Battersby.

Back at the large car park at Blakey Ridge, on a good clear day you can see almost all of the Rosedale trek to the east. The kilns at the east mines locality will be clearly visible on the far side of the dale along with the patchwork pattern of green cultivated fields on the lower slopes of the valley. Turning to face the west and this route will take us on foot to Ingleby Incline Top.

A low stone wall on the west side of the main Hutton-le-Hole to Castleton road marks the site where the railway cutting was once bridged by the road. A re-alignment of the road moved it slightly to the east along with the junction with the minor Long Lane road leading down into Farndale. At this point a 2km railway descended an incline, running almost due south, then south west to the Blakey mine and quarries in Farndale itself. These mining activities in Farndale were never as extensive as those in Rosedale as the quality of the minerals was poorer.

It is also difficult to envisage that here, near to the road bridge, were once several sidings and a row of stone cottages for the railway workers. It is said that the Victorian workforce had a harsh life here, and you do not require much imagination to sense that. This must have been a truly remarkable place to live and work in all seasons for just a pitiful wage.

The old railway route we pass over is in good condition for walking. Generally well drained, the ash surface is still the width of the old trackbed that has not seen a train for over seventy years. With a series of sharp curves, the trek follows the contours around the head of Farndale. In many ways Farndale is a similar dale to Rosedale. Running north to south it is over 10km in length with steep sides that drain into the River Dove which flows south through Kikbymoorside and into a confluence with the River Rye en route eventually to join the Derwent a few kilometres beyond Malton.

However, the section of old railway line around Farndale head was particularly exposed to the extremes of winter weather on the bleak moors. The shallow cuttings would often fill completely with drifting snow, closing the line for weeks on end.

Today only the leisurely walker, or the local game keeper, uses this level path. After a few kilometres of walking from Blakey Ridge two lonely paths cross the line of the railway, both heading from

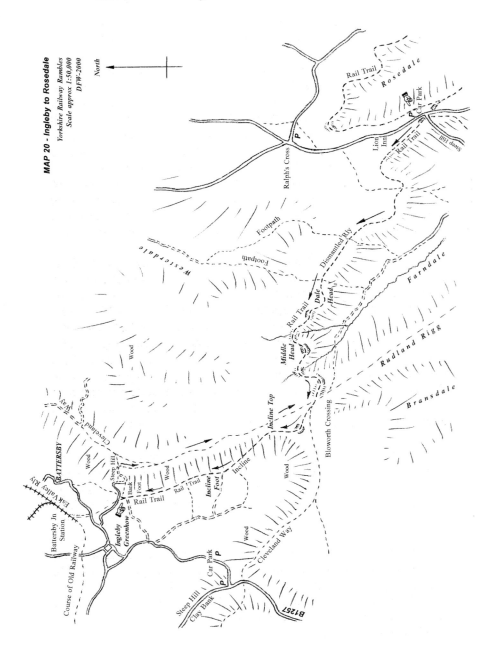

MAP 20 - Ingleby to Rosedale
Yorkshire Railway Rambles
Scale approx 1:50,000
DFW-2000

North

Farndale to Westerdale. After a rather wet cutting the line swings around to lead you almost due south before turning west again and the crossing of Rutland Rigg.

Bloworth Crossing is the location of this lonely coming of the ways. A century ago, Blakey Ridge was just the same dirt track as Rutland Rigg. To try and cross the moors with a laden cart in winter time by these old lanes is the reason that so many railways were built in seemingly inaccessible places. The railway plays host to the Lyke Wake Walk for much of its length from Blakey Ridge. Here it is also joined by the Cleveland Way as it circum navigates the moors.

You will have covered almost 10km from Blakey Ridge. It is now a further kilometre north west to the incline top, where the Cleveland Way and Lyke Wake Walk branches away to the west. The view here beyond the escarpment and over the flat plains towards Teeside is especially striking.

The many industrial sites around Teeside are north west. Clay Bank is to the west with the B1257 road from Stokesley to Helmsley labouring up the hill. In front the steep descent of Ingleby Incline cuts a straight line down the escarpment and through Battersby Plantation.

The route of the railway down the steep incline, and a further 2km on level ground, can still be followed. The path finishing about a kilometre short of the present day Battersby Junction station where the single line railway still runs north to Middlesbrough and east to Whitby. Paths can take you north to the village of Battersby and west to Ingleby Greenhow. However, for the return journey, we need to climb back up again and head east from Bank Foot back onto the moors.

A stiff climb through the forest up Ingleby Bank will raise you 175 metres in altitude and return you to the the track crossed earlier forming part of the Cleveland Way. Head right (south) walking along the top of the escarpment and 5km back to Bloworth Crossing where your original steps can be re-traced back to Blakey Ridge and the start.

It is three quarters of a century since this amazing railway has seen a locomotive. Stand amidst the landscape and you cannot help marvelling at the vision, commitment and sheer fervour of the Yorkshiremen who built and worked this standard gauge line over such difficult and formidable terrain.

How times have changed!

Fact File: Blakey Ridge to Incline Top and Battersby.

Start/Finish: Blakey Ridge car park.
Grid Refs: SE 989684. A walk over the high moors and down Ingleby Incline to Battersby.
Location: The road from Hutton-le-Hole to Castleton, 14km north of the A170 near to Kirkbymoorside.
Max. length of walk: 30km (19 miles), typical walking time 7 hours plus, Bank Foot and return.
Length of shorter walk: 20km (13 miles), typical time 5 hours, to Incline top and return.
OS maps: Landranger 93 & 94, Outdoor Leisure 26, North York Moors Western sheet.
Points of interest: Ingleby Incline, beautiful moorland scenery, spectacular views from the top of the escarpment.
Tourist information office: Hutton-le-Hole, (National Park Information Centre, seasonal opening), Tel: (01751) 417367.
Cycling: No bikes please, only walkers permitted on this trek. You will find many enjoyable routes from the car park at Blakey Ridge down into Farndale to the south west.

Walk 15 - The Guisborough Trail

It is to the north of the county that the very birth of public railways occured almost two centuries ago. The Stockton and Darlington Railway opened amidst great fanfare in 1825. Although the latter half of the eighteenth century had seen various collieries developing crude forms of railways to assist the movement of heavy raw materials and spoil in wheeled wagons, the Stockton and Darlington was different. It was a public railway to convey goods from one town to another by means of several wagons pulled by horses or a locomotive.

The promoters were exploring a totally new concept and were not quite sure how it might develop. Even the most optimistic amongst them could not have envisaged the significance of this railway, or how it was to affect firstly the whole country, then sweep around the World. Within just a few years of it opening, hundreds of railway schemes were being promoted and after a few decades, thousands of miles of tracks had beed laid to virtually every town in the country. The railway companies became the largest of employers, the greatest of land owners and the very hub of the industrial revolution that saw Britain lead the world in almost every field.

The town of Middlesbrough grew from being a small insignificant settlement into one of the great steel making centres of Europe. The docks developed rapidly, along with the chemical industry and heavy engineering. The railways helped to fuel the boom in trade along with the employment and wealth creation that went hand in hand. However, with no green belt policy or landscaping schemes in the nineteenth century the price paid was the rapid development of industrial activities at the expense of the countryside. In only a few decades the River Tees was a giant work horse with hundreds of foundries and factories along its banks. To feed the appetite of these works, raw materials shipped in by rail were required on a massive scale.

The market town of Guisborough had been a centre of the rural area for centuries and now it found itself engulfed by industrialisation. Drift mines, deep mine shafts and open quarry faces all appeared within a ten kilometre radius of the town. In that vicinity, over fifty commercial mines were being worked in the second half of the nineteenth century.

The Stockton and Darlington was originally promoted to carry coal to a wharf on the River Tees at the east side of Stockton town, however by 1830 it had extended through to Middlesbrough and steadily, along the northern coastline of the county, it reached as far as Saltburn by 1861. However as the railways expanded, Guisborough quickly gained the attentions of the companies who were keen to exploit the transhipment of thousands of tonnes of ore being mined around the town.

Thus an independent company built the Middlesbrough to Guisborough line. The route ran south from Middlesbrough through the Nunthorpe area, then east to Guisborough with a terminus station at the south side of the town centre. This opened 1854 as the number of mines rapidly increased. Another company, The Cleveland Railway reached the town in 1861, covering a route through Normanby then running parallel to the Middlesbrough and Guisborough railway to the south side of the town. Their tracks continued on through to Boosbeck, Brotton and around the coastal headland at Huntcliff to reach Skinningrove and Loftus. It was the latter part of this line that eventually become part of the coastal route through Staithes and Sandsend down to the Esk valley and Whitby.

These railways were joined by dozens of branch lines to collieries along the routes, many of which were several kilometres in length. With great rivalry between the independent companies, many changes ensued as the emerging North Eastern Railway Company steadily became the dominant player. Each of the smaller companies merged or were taken over and although the Stockton and Darlington Railway had taken control of the Middlesbrough and Guisborough Railway it itself became part of the North Eastern Railway in 1867. Just two years later and the Cleveland Railway followed its rival. The North Eastern Railway Company was now the all powerful controller of key lines in the area. One of the first acts of the North Eastern was to close the Cleveland's route to Guisborough via Normanby. Two connecting spurs were then constructed to make full use the Middlesbrough and Guisborough rails into the town. One linked the eastern section of the Cleveland Railway to Boosbeck and beyond, the other spur was at Pinchinthorpe to the west of Guisborough, where it gave access to a colliery line that would have have otherwise lost its outlet with the closure of the western section of the Cleveland line. This was all way back in the 1860s when closing duplicated railway routes on economic grounds was far from being a controversial topic.

The mineral traffic around Guisborough grew immensely. Over fifty train loads of wagons each day were hauled from the mines around the town, making the short journey to the foundries along the Tees. Although numbers would fluctuate with demand, this remained a thriving industry for well over a century. It was the quality of the ore that finally brought about the end of the Cleveland mine workings. Better quality iron ore, in greater quantities, was brought in from other areas of the country or imported through the expanding docks at Hartlepool and along the River Tees.

The mines steadily fell into decline and today the only operation in the area is the deep potash mine at Boulby. As mentioned earlier in this chapter, the Rosedale mines ceased production in the 1920s and similar activities around Grosmont finished along with many more nearer to the coast around Loftus.

The heart of the mining industry remained centred around Skelton and Guisborough and were the last to end with the final closure at

Moorland Rail Routes

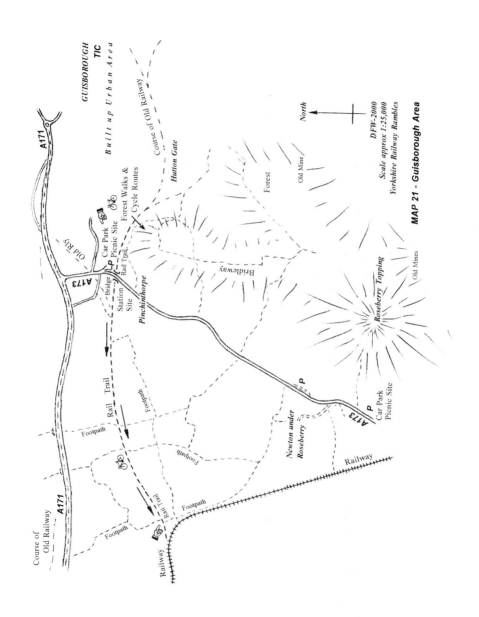

MAP 21 - Guisborough Area

Scale approx 1:25,000
Yorkshire Railway Rambles

DFW-2000

125

North Skelton in January 1964. Other than industrial traffic, railway passenger services, along with general freight traffic, had been steadily cut back in the early 1960s with Guisborough losing its service to Middlesbrough in 1963. However, not all of the route was closed and the line which had been constructed from Battersby (close to Ingleby Incline) to Nunthorpe in 1864 remained open. This line now provides the only rail link from Middlesbrough to Whitby via Battersby Junction station where the trains must change direction in order to travel east along the Esk valley via Grosmont and on to Whitby town. On this present day route, which was used to convey freight to Teeside, including the wagons from the Rosedale mines, the junction for the Guisborough line was 2km east of Nunthorpe Station.

It is over this section of track, east of the junction near Nunthorpe, travelling eastward to Pinchinthorpe and Hutton Gate to the south west of Guisborough, that this short trek has been developed.

Although this area now falls within the present day County of Cleveland, it was originally part of the County of Yorkshire which extended from south of the River Tees down to the River Humber.

The route, although short, is on the edge of the Cleveland Hills and has a succession of paths and bridleways crossing it which enable you to create longer circular routes if you desire.

With the A171 just to the north of the dismantled railway, the A173 from Great Ayton crosses over the line by Pinchinthorpe station. The main station buildings are to the west of the road bridge, with the original station (before it became a junction) at the east side. It is at this side that a car park, picnic site and nature area have been developed. Also a small visitor centre has been opened in one of the old buildings to provide further information about the area and the forest walks.

Short walks can be taken to the east along the old rail track, then south on a variety of circular forest walks and cycle routes. Alternatively, you can take a longer walk due west to the former junction with the still in use single track line to Battersby Junction. This walk can be of 6km in length, returning by the same route. By using the many paths crossing the old line, any permutation of length can be walked all the way to Roseberry Topping, 4km to the south.

A glance at the OS map will show the rich choice of footpaths and bridleways available. Although not very far from industrial Teeside, this is an excellent area for exploration with walks ranging from as little as an hours stroll right up to a full day of trekking or cycling.

Fact File: The Guisborough Trail

Start/Finish: Pinchinthorpe

Grid Refs: NZ 583152

Location: 2km west of Guisborough on A173. A pleasant walk along the railway with many circular hilly options including Roseberry Topping.

Max. length of walk: km (miles), typical walking time 2 hours, return to start.

Length of shorter walk: The choice is yours with many forest walks to select from.

OS maps: Landranger 93, Outdoor Leisure 26, North York Moors Western sheet.

Points of interest: Roseberry Topping is just to the south and is one of many excellent view points on the Cleveland Hills. All services, shops, pubs and public toilets are available in Guisborough town centre.

Tourist information office: Guisborough, (seasonal office), Tel:(01287) 633801, Middlesbrough, Tel: (01642) 264330.

Cycling: This is another 'Permissive Bridleway' as such you can cycle the full length of the dismantled railway, but please take note of any council restrictions that may be applied. There are several bridleways to the south of this trek that will enable you to make a hilly circular route up onto the moors, south of Hutton Village.

By the same author

Yorkshire Wolds Wanderings

ISBN 0 9507960 4 2   £6.95

An excellent pocket guide book for walkers, cyclists and motorists wanting to explore the history and natural beauty of this unspoilt and undiscovered corner of England.

Includes twenty detailed route maps and illustrated with attractive pen and ink sketches of notable landmarks and places of interest.

Santona Publications
Rydal Mount
224 Marlborough Avenue
Hull HU5 3LE   Tel: 01482 441021